GW00372262

Robin Matthews
July 2004

Cambridge
June 2001

THE
HIMALAYAS

A WORD TO THE READER

The transcription of Indian and Tibetan languages into English poses the usual problems
one encounters in going from a phonetic writing to an orthographic writing.
With the inevitable imprecisions due to the complexity of the Indian languages
the pronunciation system adopted in this book is the following:
VOWELS: to simplify matters, no distinction is made between long and short vowels
a is pronounced as in "watch"
i is pronounced as in "ski"
o is pronounced as in "no"
e is pronounced as a shortened diphthong form of "day"
u is pronounced as in "you"
ai is pronounced as in "bed"
au is pronounced approximately as the above-mentioned "a" and "o"
CONSONANTS: to simplify matters, all consonants with diacritical signs that only slightly modify
their sound for an English ear have been assimilated to the simple, corresponding consonants
b, d, k, l, m, n, p, q, r, s, v are pronounced as in English
y is pronounced as in "ski"
g is always heard as in "go"
ch is pronounced as in "chair"
h is always aspirated as in "home"
n is pronounced as in the last syllable of "pneumonia"
bh, chh, dh, gh, jh, kh, ph are all aspirates
sh (which transcribes both the subscript sh and the superscript sh) is pronounced as in "shelf"
The Tibetan languages include "silent" letters which are not pronounced.
Some authors have chosen to transliterate all the letters, others have eliminated some
or all of the "silent" letters, which explains the extreme complexity of the systems and
the innumerable quarrels. In this book, the system adopted for Tibetan names and expressions
is a phonetic transcription (and sometimes a partial transliteration) intended to facilitate English
pronunciation. Therefore, most of the sounds should be pronounced as in English.

THE HIMALAYAS

TEXTS AND PHOTOGRAPHS:
ALAIN CHENEVIÈRE

TRANSLATED BY
LENORE MALTZ-RIGUET

Directed by Roger SABATER

Table of contents

8
Introduction

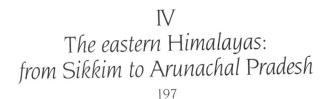

Whether you approach by land or fly over them, the Himalayas always appear as a great mountain system bearing the stamp of the infinite. Only superlatives are adequate to describe them. The Himalayas are the greatest mountain chain in the world; they are also the vastest, the longest and the highest, including

happily after discovering the fountain of youth. Obviously, no one has ever found the valley, nor encountered the gods, the genies or the giant ants (though some think that in the accounts told to Herodotus, they may have been mistaken for marmots). And yet, the magic of the Himalayas has captivated people over the centuries. Still to this

Introduction

the fourteen "twenty-sixers" which compose the "Roof of the World". In the Himalayas one finds the largest glaciers, the deepest valleys, the most vertiginous elevation differences and the most extreme climates. Since the dawn of time, men have been either captivated or terrified by these giant mountains and have imagined that hidden within them was a mysterious domain defended by impenetrable rock walls. The great Indian epics, the *Mahabharata* and the *Ramayana* already mentioned the existence in northern India of high mountain chains inhabited by gods, genies and demons. In 430 BC Herodotus, the respectable Greek historian hardly prone to exaggeration, unhesitatingly asserted that the western part of these same mountains harbored giant ants tirelessly digging away for gold in the many mines of the region.

Later, the myth of Shangri La enchanted whole generations. Immortal men were said to live there

day, the lofty peaks and the mysterious valleys continue to fascinate all those who approach. The majesty of the region adds to the peculiar sense of awe the Himalayas inspire in those who live there, as well as in those who pass through.

For Hindus and Buddhists, Indians, Nepalese and Tibetans, this is the site of the earth's axis, the mythical Mount Meru or Mandara which was the pivot for the gods as they churned the primeval Ocean of Milk. The many *ashrams* located on the slopes of the holy mountain provide a haven where monks, hermits and ascetics pursue their mystical quests and meditation. The "purest" of these sages find refuge in grottos or even at the foot of the glaciers. Each hill, each peak and each river has its history, its succession of legends and is home to a deity. More and more foreigners come to these sites that, ever since childhood, have nourished their dreams. And they discover that the reality is even more extraordinary than what they had imagined. The Himalayan chain is always higher than they believed, always vaster, always more beautiful. Many people set out to climb the un-scaled peaks of the Himalayas to get closer to heaven; finally, even the "twenty-sixers" were conquered. The era of the discoverers is over;

that of the explorer is finishing. Today is the era of trekkers and tourists. Will they have as much res-pect as their predecessors did for these giant mountains at the junction of Europe, China and India? Will our "civilized" world know how to avoid polluting the last haven of the gods?

The Himalayas are an extraordinary set of young, living mountains that , despite intense erosion, are constantly rising. It is undoubtedly this profound feeling of intense life that troubles and seduces mankind. Whoever sets foot on Himalayan ground experiences this confused effervescence. Believers see in it a sign of one or several gods; agnostics feel close to pure, all-powerful nature. Here beau-ty and the sublime commingle with the mystical and the magical. No one returns from the Hima-layas unchanged. He who has seen and "felt" this fabulous realm will never again see things in the same light.

View of the chain one early February morning. The peaks emerge slowly out of the mist. One understands why the people who live here consider the Himalayas the abode of the Gods.

A traditional village, ▶ typical of the Zangla valley in Kinnaur. The timber and stone houses are covered with slate roofs and grouped around their fort on a rocky fortified promontory which overhangs the river.

A Description of the Himalayan Region

The Himalayans separate the Tibetan high plateaus from the Indo-Gangetic alluvial plain. By their dimension and mass they are the largest mountain chain on earth. They are shaped like an enormous crescent, 1,600 miles long and from 155 to 250 miles wide, mainly oriented northwest southeast, then west northeast, and finally ending on both sides by an abrupt fold towards the south from which the Afghan Hindu Kush range angles off to the west and the Chinese Longsmanshan mass to the east.

The glaciers of the Tirish Mir range which reach their highest point at 25,325 feet supply water to a whole network of valleys where shepherd populations live. Winter weather closes the passes and blocks off the whole region for more than four months.

The Western Himalayas . The splendid Kulu valley known as "the Valley
of the Gods, "in which the Beas winds, is between 8,200 feet and 9,800 feet
in altitude.In the 2nd century this fertile valley was the seat of a Hindu state;
then it became a Tibetan fief in the 11th century, before it developed economically
under the Rajput kings beginning in the 18th century.

The southern central Himalayas. Aerial view of Everest as seen from
the east, in winter. At the bottom right, through the openings of the glacial
valleys can be seen the border of the Tibetan plateau which comes
to rest against the mountains.

The highest mountain chain on earth

The Himalayan mountain system is located between 27° and 35° latitude north, which places it in the intertropical zone. The sheer size of the mountains, however, has produced a surprising variety of climatic stages. Finally, the orientation of the chains which conditions exposure to monsoons or stops the rains, has resulted in a wide variety of zones, ranging from very hot, humid forests to arid, freezing deserts. The Himalayas are, thus, the region of the world that experiences the greatest climatic variations.

The Himalayas fascinate both geographers and geologists, for they are the perfect and unique example of a collision chain, formed by the encounter of two continental lithospheres. Geographers are in the habit of subdividing the Himalayan range longitudinally into three zones characterized by large, parallel mountainous axes. From south to north one encounters first the Siwalik range, followed to the west by the Murree range which is never more than twenty-five miles wide and whose tallest peaks vary between 2,600 and 5,000 feet in height. Next one comes to the border range, known as the Lesser Himalayas or Mahabharat Lekh, which is wider (around 50 miles) and higher (the average altitude is close to 9,000 feet). Finally, the enormous barrier of the Great Himalayas and the Transhimalayas (which the Chinese call the Gandisi chain) loom up, most of whose peaks are above 20,000 feet and harbor the 14 giants of the earth, culminating at over 26,000 feet. This zone varies greatly from 60 to 150 miles in width.

Geologists accept this division which corresponds to a coherent plan of geological formation. The first chain of mountains corresponds to the sub-Himalayan zone, with its recent deposits. The second and the third constitute the actual Himalayan zone, with its very distorted sedimentary and metamorphic series. Geographers, however, prefer to distinguish four transversal Himalayan zones within the range, limited by the major rivers.

From west to east, then, one finds the Karakorum-Punjab Himalayas (approximately 460 miles from Yarkhun to the Sutlej), the Kumaon Himalayas (217 miles from the Sutlej to the Kali), the Nepalese Himalayas (500 miles from the Kali to the Tista), and the Himalayas of Assam (435 miles from the Tista to the Brahmaputra).

Without exploring the geological structure of these zones in detail, it is useful to recall the main rock formations one comes across in the Himalayas. First, those of the continental crust, which constitute four-fifths of the chain. There are always two distinct parts: the very old Precambrian substratum (which corresponds to the Indian shield) and the blanket of marine sediments, banked up from the Paleozoic to the beginning of the Cenozoic age. Then comes the oceanic crust which is represented by ophiolite rocks, covered by sediments, in the subduction zones (Ladakh, Tsangpo, Shyok, Anduo, etc.) and finally a type of intermediary crust in which are piled up, starting at the bottom, a first series of infracrustal rocks or the upper mantle, a second series of metamorphic igneous rocks and the third, a basalt effusion covered by marine sediments from the Cretaceous era.

The biggest water tower on earth

All the major rivers that flow through the Indian sub-continent and Tibet have their source in the Himalayas, whose orography is as distinctive as their other features. Indeed, the watershed does not correspond to the crest line, as it does everywhere else. It is located some 100 miles further north at the southern border of the Tibetan plateau.

By a peculiar geological accident, the early hydrographic system, which existed prior to Himalayan orogeny, survived the great uplifts. This explains the existence of the narrowest, deepest gorges on earth, such as those of the Sutlej, the Arun, the Brahmaputra (called Yarlong Tsangpo in Tibet) which flow 20,000 feet below Namcha Barva and Gyala Peri, and especially the Kali Gandaki, deeply embanked at the foot of Dhaulagiri (26,811 feet), with its world record depth of 7,546 feet. It is believed that the very powerful pre-Himalayan rivers were able to maintain their courses despite the convulsions of a mountain that was, and still is, rising at the exceptional rate of two and three-quarters to four inches a year (excluding erosion).

These early rivers must have run southward, towards the Thetys. As the mountains rose and became an obstacle to be skirted, they flowed westward or eastward for hundreds of miles (for example, the Ganges and the Brahmaputra for over 1,000 miles) before bending abruptly southward when the opportunity of a gap in the wall of mountains arose. For millions of years, the rivers cut deeply into the mountain sides, and by scraping the river beds and banks, and by freeing great quantities of water that gouged the facades of the chain, rounded into a "U" the bed that Quaternary glaciers had cut into a "V".

A cultural, religious and racial crossroads

The Himalayas are the main junction between the Indo-European world and the Asian world. Their high valleys were settled much later. At the present time, we do not possess any evidence that man lived in the the Lesser or Great Himalayas before our era. On the other hand, human sites, over 500,000 years old, have been found on the sides of the Siwalik Hills. The Tibetan peoples and others of Mongoloid origin akin to them, colonized the high plateau north of the Himalayan chain as early as the Paleolithic Age and made

An extraordinary geographical entity

their way up the eastern and western steps at the beginning of the Neolithic Age.

To the south, the Indo-European populations began entering the western Himalayan region approximately twenty centuries ago. Less than three hundred years later they were permanently settled on the entire Indo-Gangetic piedmont and on many of the southern

The Aryans and the Tibetans met and conquered indigenous Negrito type populations in the west and Dravidians in the east, about whom we have very little information, except that they were not warlike and had dark skin. The aborigines now living in Kashmir and Nepal are undoubtedly their descendants. There was very little intermingling between them and the

slopes of the chain. The term "Indo-European" refers more to a linguistic entity (from western Europe to the Indian sub-continent, and including Scandinavia, the Slavic world and the Turco-Irano-Afghan regions) than to a strict ethnic reality. The Indo-Europeans are believed to have originated somewhere in the immense steppes and forests south of present-day Russia and to have begun emigrating south and west thirty centuries ago. Five centuries later, they had crossed the Danube and had arrived in the Middle East. Three centuries after that, they had entered Mesopotamia and had reached the Iranian plateau. It is here that a group broke away and called themselves Aryans ("arya" means "nobles") to mark themselves off from the defeated populations they called Anarya ("non-nobles"). In 1500 BC these "nobles" reached the Himalayas.

warlike invaders from the northeast and the west, who were interested in preserving their racial purity.

On the Asian side, however, the mixing of certain Tibetan groups with the local population gave birth to many Tibeto-Burmese ethnic groups of the central and eastern Himalayas. In Arunachal Pradesh, the situation is complicated, due to the influence of other non-Tibetan Mongoloid peoples.

The wealth of the successive human contributions in the Himalayan region has brought about an exceptional mosaic of cultures and languages, dominated by the Brahman and Tibetan civilizations. The essence of each of these has found its best expression in the philosophical or religious doctrines of Hinduism and Buddhism, both of which have become world religions. With the advent of Islam, which came from the west in

The northern central Himalayas. The high plateau of Tibet is like an old eroded, flattened platform folded by thrusts of the Himalayan mass which is in constant upheaval. Certain parts of this vast, particularly dry and arid territory are sand deserts; as here, north of Tsedang.

The Subansiri is one of the main massifs of the eastern Lesser Himalayas.
Up against the giant walls of the central chain, subject to a very humid climate,
it looks like a succession of big blocks of mountains covered with thick vegetation.

the 10th century, the Himalayas became the meeting place of three of the greatest cultures and religions of the world.

More than forty million people live, unevenly distributed, within the Himalayan region. Most of them lead sedentary lives in the lowlands and the valleys under 10,000 feet altitude. The upper regions are sparsely inhabited, mostly by nomads earning their living from animal raising. Several countries and large regions are partially or totally located within the Himalayas. From west to east there are Pakistan (the northern part of the North-West Border Province, including Azad Kashmir), the northwest of India (Jammu and Kashmir, Himachal Pradesh, the northern part of Uttar Pradesh), Nepal, southern Tibet, Sikkim (a state that joined the Indian Union in 1975), Bhutan and the northeast of India (Arunachal Pradesh and the northern part of Assam).

The Indus between Skardu and Gol at the beginning of a very light July monsoon. Despite the water from the melting glaciers one can see the big granitic rocks and the morainic debris which clutter up the bed of this powerful river.

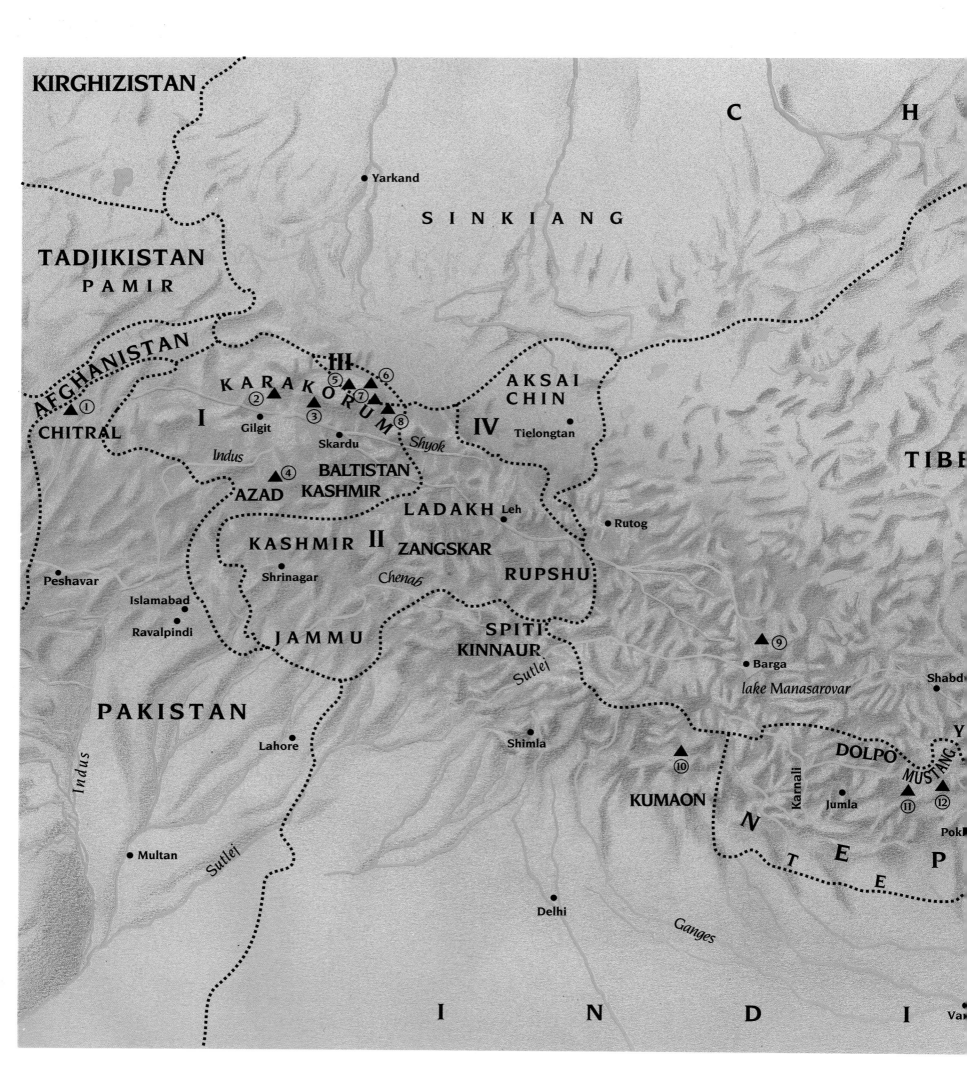

KIRGHIZISTAN

C   H

SINKIANG

● Yarkand

TADJIKISTAN

PAMIR

AFGHANISTAN

KARAKORUM

III

⑤ ▲
② ▲   ⑥ ▲
⑦ ▲

▲ ①

CHITRAL

I

● Gilgit

③ ▲

⑧ ▲

AKSAI
CHIN

IV

● Tielongtan

TIBE

● Skardu   Shyok

Indus

▲ ④

AZAD

BALTISTAN

KASHMIR

LADAKH   ● Leh

● Peshavar

KASHMIR   II   ZANGSKAR

● Rutog

● Shrinagar   Chenab

RUPSHU

● Islamabad

● Ravalpindi

JAMMU

SPITI

KINNAUR

▲ ⑨

● Barga

● Shabd

lake Manasarovar

PAKISTAN

Sutlei

● Lahore

● Shimla

DOLPO

Y

▲ ⑩

MUSTANG

Karnali

● Jumla

KUMAON

▲ ⑪   ▲ ⑫

● Pok

N

● Multan   Sutlei

E

T

E

P

I   N   D   I

● Delhi

Ganges

● Var

22

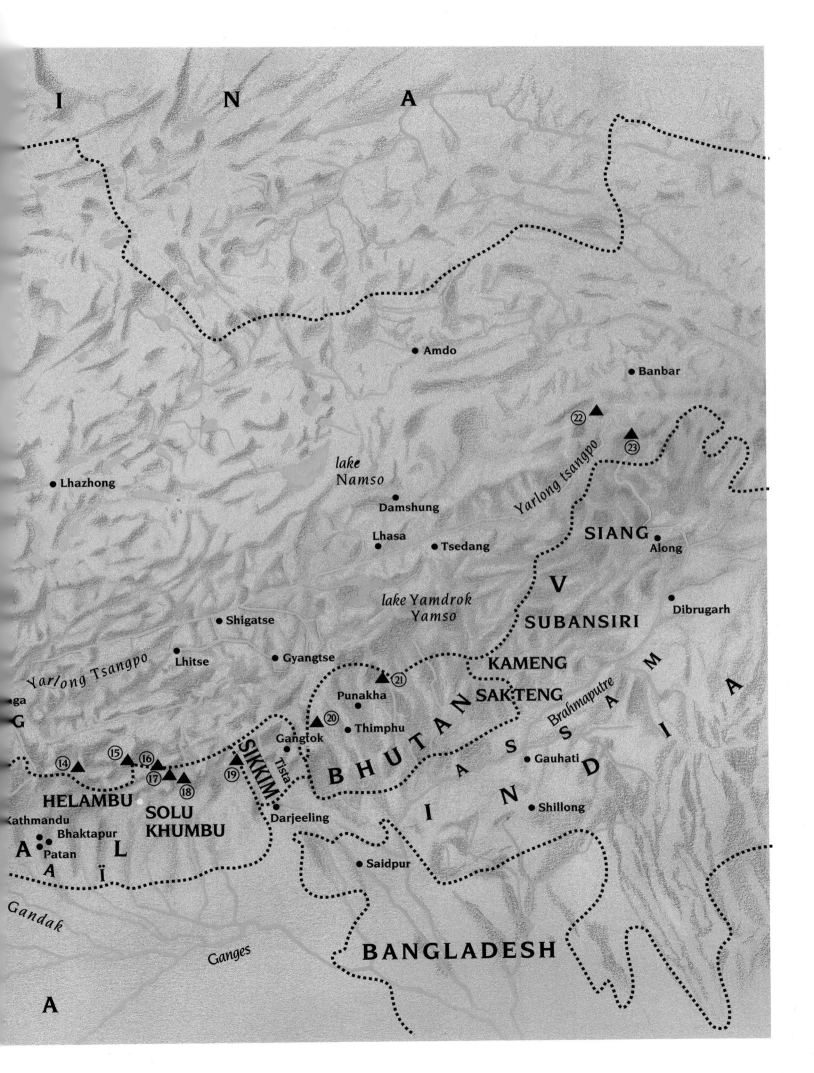

① Tirish Mir (25,325 ft)

② Rakaposhi (25,558 ft)

③ Haramosh (24,212 ft)

④ Nanga Parbat
(26,660 ft)

⑤ K2 (28,251 ft)

⑥ Broad Peak
(26,400 ft)

⑦ Gasherbrum II
(26,361 ft)

⑧ Gasherbrum I
(26,469 ft)

⑨ Kailasa (22,028 ft)

⑩ Nanda Devi
(25,643 ft)

⑪ Dhaulagiri (26,811 ft)

⑫ Annapurna
(26,545 ft)

⑬ Manaslu (26,781 ft)

⑭ Shisha Pangma
(26,299 ft)

⑮ Cho Oyu (26,749 ft)

⑯ Everest (29,029 ft)

⑰ Lhotse (27,940 ft)

⑱ Makalu (27,766 ft)

⑲ Kanchenjunga
(28,215 ft)

⑳ Chomolhari
(23,996 ft)

㉑ Kula Khangri
(24,948 ft)

㉒ Namcha Barva
(25,446 ft)

㉓ Gyala Peri (23,461 ft)

I, II, III, IV, V :
Zones claimed
by the different
countries.

23

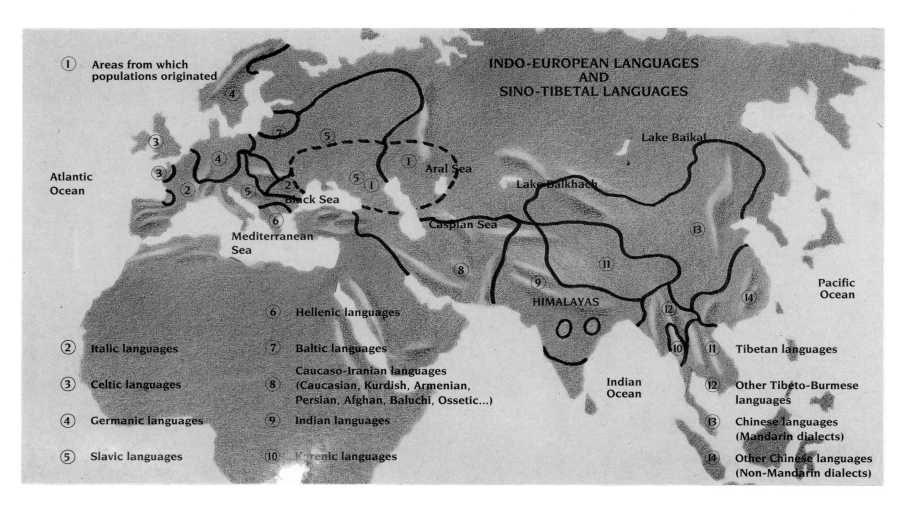

**INDO-EUROPEAN LANGUAGES
AND
SINO-TIBETAL LANGUAGES**

① Areas from which populations originated

Atlantic Ocean

Lake Baikal

Aral Sea

Lake Balkhach

Black Sea

Caspian Sea

Mediterranean Sea

HIMALAYAS

Pacific Ocean

Indian Ocean

② Italic languages

③ Celtic languages

④ Germanic languages

⑤ Slavic languages

⑥ Hellenic languages

⑦ Baltic languages

⑧ Caucaso-Iranian languages (Caucasian, Kurdish, Armenian, Persian, Afghan, Baluchi, Ossetic...)

⑨ Indian languages

⑩ Karenic languages

⑪ Tibetan languages

⑫ Other Tibeto-Burmese languages

⑬ Chinese languages (Mandarin dialects)

⑭ Other Chinese languages (Non-Mandarin dialects)

A shy Gaddi nomad from Azad Kashmir.

A young Kalash woman fron the Bumboret valley in Chitral.

A Kinnauri storekeeper from Kanum in Himachal Pradesh.

A Nepalese of the Nevar ethnic group from the Kathmandu valley.

Tibetan shepherds from the Bomi region are related to the Khampa of Namdo.

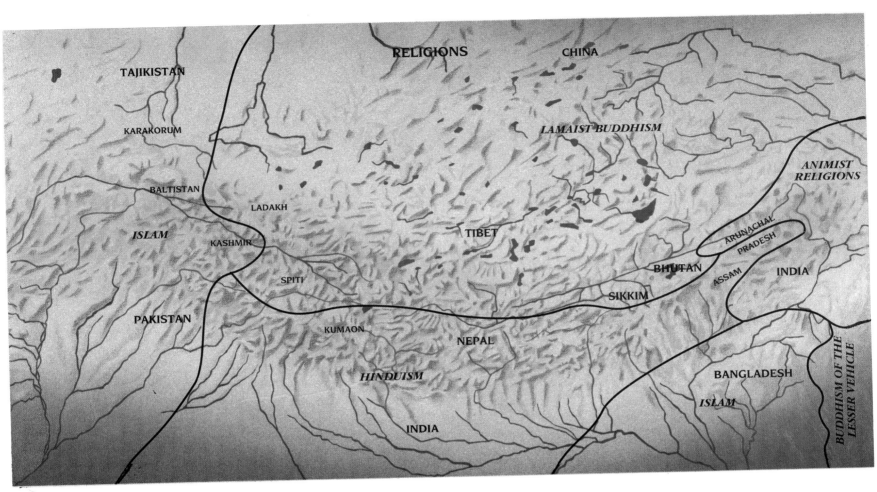

RELIGIONS

TAJIKISTAN

KARAKORUM

BALTISTAN

LADAKH

ISLAM KASHMIR

SPITI

PAKISTAN

KUMAON

HINDUISM

INDIA

CHINA

LAMAIST BUDDHISM

ANIMIST RELIGIONS

TIBET

ARUNACHAL PRADESH

BHUTAN ASSAM INDIA

SIKKIM

NEPAL

BANGLADESH

ISLAM

BUDDHISM OF THE LESSER VEHICLE

A young aristocratic Bhutanese woman belonging to the Nyos clan from Bumthang.

An Indian peasant from Kumaon in northern Uttar Pradesh.

Tea picker belonging to an Adivasi ethnic group from southern Kameng related to the early Bengalese.

A Zangskari man from Yuldo in Ladakh.

A woman from the semi-nomadic ethnic group, the Adi, in Siang.

25

The steps of the Tibetan plateau here in Rupshu are incised by deep valleys
dug by rivers originating on the northern slope of the Himalayas.
After following the central range, these rivers plunge southward once
the slope has made it possible to find a gap.

It all began 250 million years ago, at the end of the primary era. A single continent existed on the planet; it was called Pangaea. Under the influence of the powerful convectional forces that constantly move the earth's mantle, Pangaea divided into two supercontinents, Laurasia in the north and Gondwana in the south –although, of course, these notions of north and south are purely hypothetical, since they take into account the present magnetic pole of the earth which reverses itself at irregular intervals. Over the last 75 million years, there have been 171 changes in polarity. Consequently, one cannot decisively assert that, at that moment, Laurasia was at the north and Gondwana at the south. These are simply working hypotheses which are practical for locating the continents on a map of the world.

A chain of mountains born beneath the sea

Laurasia and Gondwana were separated by an immense 3,700-mile-wide sea, called Thetys. Laurasia remained relatively stable, at the same latitude, whereas Gondwana, which was to become the future Antarctica, Africa, Australia and India, to mention only some, was constantly moving northward and cracking. India occupied its northeastern part. What was to become the Himalayas was still beneath the waters of the Thetys and their future location, also beneath the sea, was piling up sediments carried by the great rivers of paleo-Asia.

Starting 200 million years ago Gondwana broke up permanently. Because of their mass, the future major continents separated more slowly than the microcontinents, which escaped towards the edge of the lithospheric plates. This is what happened to the two "pieces" of Tibet (which we shall call Tibet I and Tibet II) that, during the Permian age, settled, one by one, up against the Asian continent: for Tibet I, around 160 million years ago and for Tibet II, 80 million years ago. These mini-collisions produced a series of low mountain ranges that undulate across the Asian topography.

Certain subduction zones, veritable scars on the earth's surface, indicate the contact zones between the Asian continent and Tibet I, on the one hand (the south-Kunlunshan subduction zone), and Tibet I and Tibet II, on the other hand (the Anduo or Bangong Nujiang subduction zone).

Meanwhile, once the Indian Ocean had opened, the enormous Indian mass broke off from Africa (between 120 and 80 million years ago). The Indian continent, "floating" on the mantle, drifted in a northeasterly direction towards Asia at the considerable speed of four to seven and three-quarter inches per year. This means that over a period of ten million years India covered 900 miles –a unique feat in the history of the earth for a continent of this size! The denser Indian ocean plate

The geological history of the Himalayas

progressively sank under the Asian continental plate, causing a narrowing of the Thetys, compensated for by an equivalent broadening of the Indian Ocean.

The frontal shock of the two continental lithospheres

The veritable collision between India and Asia took place around 45 million years ago. The sudden dip of the Indian oceanic lithosphere into the asthenosphere was possible because of the existence of several subduction zones in southern Laurasia. Two are known precisely. One is located at the present southern Tibetan border where an "Andean type" mountain chain, characterized by intense volcanic activity causing a deepening of the Thetysian depths at its southern edges, formed. The second corresponds to the Ladakh and Kohistan arc. This arc, which is characterized by highly distorted layers and a great number of ophiolites, reveals a central width over sixty miles long, which proves that this is where the first impact was produced, when the Indian continent came to set itself diagonally into Asia, some 60 to 70 million years ago.

When the two continents joined, the Thetys disappeared, leaving, as the only sign of its existence, the Tsangpo subduction zone, containing the upper courses of the Indus and the Tsangpo. The shock between the two continent plates was colossal. The tortured facies of the geological layers, sheared by gigantic overthrusts, themselves broken by traverse faults, attest to the violence of the collision. The deeply buried metamorphic rocks resurfaced, whereas the upper layers, as they came face to face were violently folded. Their movements affected the Thetysian marine sediments and the sediments carried by the pre-Himalayan rivers. Brutally distorted and metamorphisized by the combined actions of heat and compression, these sediments, along with the metamorphic rocks spit up from the entrails of the earth, were forced southward and stacked up on the southern border of India. Less often, they were carried back towards the north. This is so in Ladakh, where the Indian continent overlaps the ophiolites on the Asian continent. Here, the Tibetan plateau was raised (its average altitude is 14,700 feet) and large mountain ranges were formed. Located behind the Himalayas are the present ranges: to the north, the Kunlunshans (which reach 23,891 feet), to the west, the Pamirs (which reach 24,590 feet) and to the east, the Longmanshans (24,902 feet).

One theory shared by most scientists today offers an explanation for this unprecedented geological upset. The Indian continental lithosphere was undoubtedly slowed by its encounter with Asia, but continued, inexorably, to move at an estimated rate of between two and two and three-quarter inches a year. It is thus accepted that the lower portion of this crust continued to descend into the asthenosphere under Asia, whereas the upper portion, which was too light to slip below was "planed off" by the Asian rim. It broke off from the deeper portion, fragmented into successive plates that reared up and remained above the intercontinental subduction zone, before piling up and considerably deepening the continental crust (up to 47 miles in the Great Himalayas).

While in the north, the "harder" Asian front broke into giant continental blocks that slid one on top of the other, causing serious earthquakes, to the south, the "softer" Indian front, changed shape, folding back on itself as it rose. At certain times the pressures were so strong that the Indian continental crust cracked and broke up into giant strips that folded back on it. Metamorphosed rocks came up to the surface from great depths to close the faults, solidifying them all into one immense, compact block. It is to this phenomenon that the Himalayas owe their origin. A first fault was produced between 30 and 15 million years ago and brought about the emergence of the Great Himalayas where the highest summits can be found. The molasse produced by severe erosion then began to form at the foot of the Indian piedmont. That is where the second fault occurred approximately 10 million years ago. Responding to the enormous southward thrust of the continental crust, the southern rim of the Great Himalayas folded back down on its piedmont. The latter, folded and broken, rose up in successive folds like giant stairways from south to north, forming first the border chain of the Mahabharat Lekhs, then the Siwaliks. Two large subduction zones indicate this double fracture in the continental crust: the central overthrust fold (MCT) which separates the Great Himalayas from the Lesser Himalayas and the border overthrust fold (MBT) before the Siwaliks. This is a zone of intense seismic activity that often has catastrophic consequences.

A continuing uplift

Is that the end of the Himalayas' history? Obviously not, for the Indian continental lithosphere is inexorably moving, leading to a constant rising of its mass and the appearance of new reliefs. Other faults are already in preparation south of the Siwaliks, where, in several millions of years, new Himalayan ridges will emerge. The Himalayan chain is alive. It is growing by an average of between three-hundredths of an inch and four-tenths of an inch per year, despite the effects of intense erosion which is unceasingly wearing away at the mountains by means of rain, wind, ice and snow. The Indian oceanic lithosphere is thus going to continue to dip under Asia, raising the entire Himalayas and extending itself towards the south. If one were to credit current data, it is quite possible to assert that India will have completely disappeared in some 50 million years. As for the immediate future, geophysicists con-sider that all the Himalayan zones will be subject to at least one earthquake of great intensity within the next one hundred to one hundred and fifty years.

But nature sometimes has surprises in store for us. At the present time the Himalayan range is the theater of two types of contradictory forces. Its western and eastern edges, as well as practically the entire Lesser Himalayas continue to rise, pushed by enormous deep forces. On the other hand, southern Tibet and the entire northern section of the Great Himalayas, which constitutes too great a continental mass for its power to be restrained horizontally, seem to be coming apart and collapsing, through the action of surface forces such as the watercourses, glaciers and earthquakes. The future of the whole range can be summarized in a simple question. Which forces will win? those from the depths or those from the surface? If it is the former, the Himalayas will continue to rise. If it is the latter, the range will be fragmented into blocks that will gradually be reduced into medium-sized secondary chains tossed, as it were, to the side, as if victims of a fateful elevation limit. According to current knowledge and recent, albeit limited, fieldwork, the second theory seems to be favored by specialists.

FORMATION OF THE HIMALAYAN CHAIN ▶

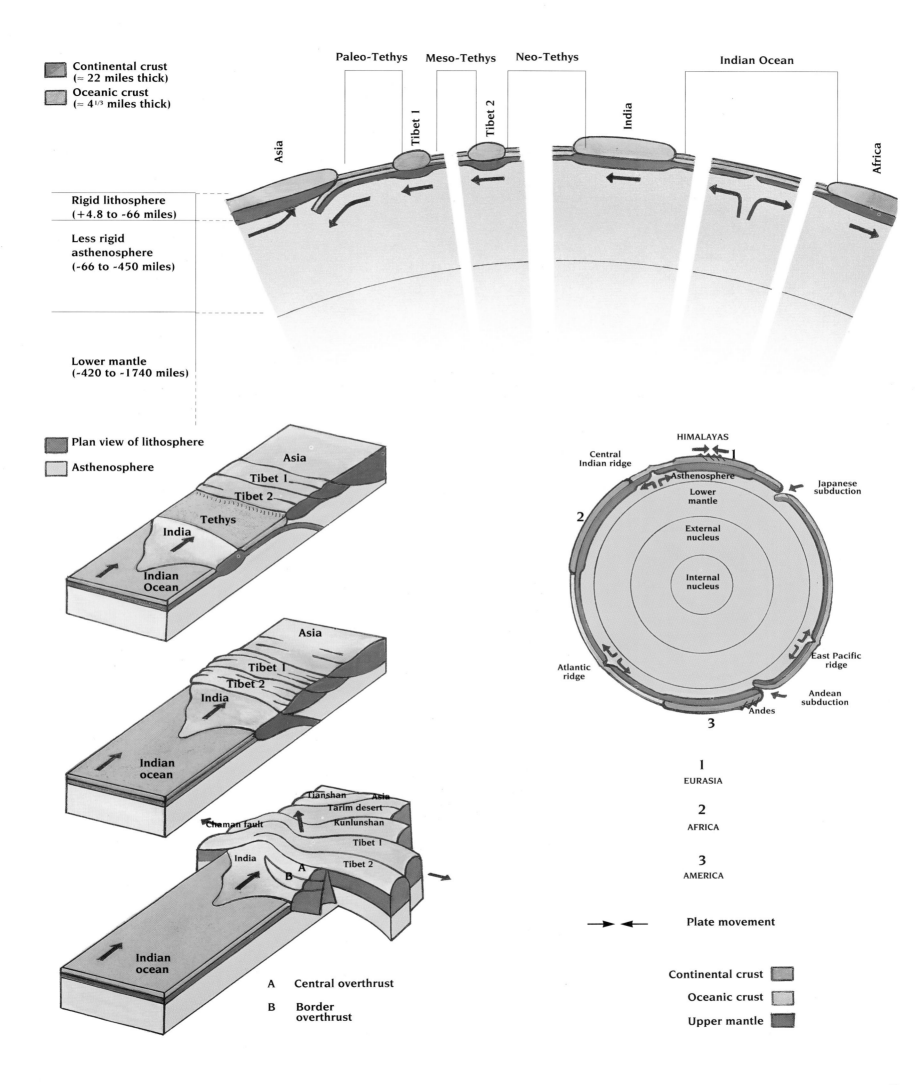

Continental crust
(≈ 22 miles thick)

Oceanic crust
(≈ 4¹/³ miles thick)

Paleo-Tethys Meso-Tethys Neo-Tethys   Indian Ocean

Asia

Tibet 1

Tibet 2

India

Africa

Rigid lithosphere
(+4.8 to -66 miles)

Less rigid
asthenosphere
(-66 to -450 miles)

Lower mantle
(-420 to -1740 miles)

Plan view of lithosphere

Asthenosphere

Asia
Tibet 1
Tibet 2
Tethys
India
Indian
Ocean

Asia
Tibet 1
Tibet 2
India
Indian
ocean

Tianshan   Asia
Tarim desert
Chaman fault   Kunlunshan
India   Tibet 1
         A   Tibet 2
         B

Indian
ocean

A   Central overthrust

B   Border
     overthrust

HIMALAYAS

Central
Indian ridge   Asthenosphere

Lower
mantle   Japanese
                 subduction
External
nucleus

2   Internal
                 nucleus

Atlantic
ridge
                          East Pacific
                          ridge
Andean
subduction
                 Andes
3

1
EURASIA

2
AFRICA

3
AMERICA

→ ← Plate movement

Continental crust

Oceanic crust

Upper mantle

29

A wild rose bush (Rosa webbiana) *from Spiti. This common bush with long thorns grows between altitudes of 4,900 to 13,100 feet in the rocky terrain from southern Pakistan to western Nepal. It can reach 8 feet in height.*

Some of the richest flora of the planet can be found in the Himalayas. Several tens of thousands of species have already been identified although most of Arunachal Pradesh, at the eastern side of the range and covered with luxuriant vegetation, has yet to be studied. This exceptional abundance is due to a unique combination of three factors: the junction of the Indian and Eurasian plates, the geographical position of the Himalayas and the particularly high, long morphology of the mountain system.

The Himalayan "jumble"

The Himalayan flora is distinguished by the exceptional variety of species and by their surprising proliferation. It is estimated, for instance, that there are at least 7,000 species of flowering plants. On the one hand, the Indo-Eurasian collision saw to it that plants belonging to two very different worlds were brought together, then dispersed, and then intermingled. Here can be found the explanation for the surprising number of species. On the other hand, the Himalayan chain combines and even accentuates by its sheer size, the effects of latitude and altitude. Its location, in the middle of a hot, humid intertropical zone, subject to monsoons, creates ideal climatic conditions for the development of plant life. What is more, the extent of the Himalayan area, whose average altitude is 6,500 feet higher than that of the Andes, the second highest chain, provides the various species with a practically unlimited domain in which to find a suitable terrain, from the orchid to the milk-vetch (locoweed). Finally, the length and the curve of the Himalayan crescent have played a determining role. Between the eastern and western sides, there is not only a distance of 1,680 miles, but also a difference of 8° in latitude, which corresponds to the variation between London and Genoa! Hence, it is understandable that there should be numerous and very noticeable differences between the west which is extremely dry, and the humidity-saturated east.

Each climatic stage is thus constantly subject to two simultaneous and complex influences, one vertical, and the other, horizontal. This situation is even more complicated, due to the many micro-climates, the limits of each area being set by the surrounding mountains. This all contributes to the impression that the vegetation is "untidy" and too rich, which has led most specialists to use the word "jumble" to define the Himalayan flora.

The different climatic stages and their vegetation

All the above elements contribute to the difficulties experts have in fitting the Himalayas into the standard pattern of climatic stages, each one with a uniform type of vegetation. Nevertheless, I hope the reader will

The flora

pardon my reducing the Himalayas to ten comprehensive climato-botanical stages –the Alps have only five– including the presence of a high altitude tropical forest and an upper limit of tree growth as high as 14,760 feet, whereas in the Alps the timberline is at around 10,500 feet.

The lowlands and the foothills between 655 and 3,300 feet form the tropical region, followed by the low mountains (3,200 feet to 4,900 feet) of the subtropical zone. Next come the middle mountains of 4,900 to 6,500 feet in the hot temperate zone; then, the warm temperate zone from 6,500 to 8,500 feet and the cold temperate zone, from 8,500 to 10,500 feet. Above this begin the high and very high mountain regions. There are, successively, the subalpine zone from 10,500 to 12,500 feet, the lower alpine zone from 12,500 to 14,000 feet, and the upper alpine zone from 14,000 to 16,000 feet. The subnivean zone is from 16,000 to 18,000 feet, then the nival zone that continues to the summits. These altitudes correspond to a general average for the Himalayas. However, as we have seen, these characteristics vary greatly from one end of the range to the other. Therefore, in the west, the upper limits of each stage must be reduced by approximately 2,600 to 3,200 feet, and, conversely, raised by as much in the east.

It is impossible to draw up a complete list of Himalayan plant species, about many of which we know little. The eastern regions, in particular, have hardly been explored and certainly reserve a goodly number of surprises. Those which have been identified already reach tens of thousands. We shall thus group the different climatic stages into four "super-stages": the tropical (tropical and subtropical), the temperate (hot, warm and cold), the alpine (subalpine, upper and lower alpine), and the snow (nival and subnivean) stages, and present for each of them the principal dominant species.

The tropical zone

The tropical and subtropical stages can be distinguished by the presence of dense forests dominated by tall plants and trees, such as the sal (*Shorea robusta*) with its graceful trunk whose hard wood is greatly appreciated by craftsmen, the banyan (*Ficus benghalensis*), a fig tree with aerial adventitious roots, and the pipal (*Ficus religiosa*), another fig tree with very light heart-shaped leaves. These trees have two features in common: they grow alone and lose their leaves every three months.

One also finds palm trees (*Phoenix sylvestris*), pandanus (*Pandanus nepalensis*), many varieties of bamboo (*Dendrocalamus hamiltonii*, D. *strictus*, D. *hookeri*, *Bambusa nutans*), especially in the Terai and Arunachal Pradesh, as well as trees that flower in the spring, such as the simal (*Bombax ceiba*),commonly called the "kapok tree", whose trunk is furnished with big thorns and large, bright red flowers, the bauhinia (Bauhinia purpurea, B. variegata), with their "camel's foot" leaves, and the caesalpinia (Caesalpinia decapetala) with its cluster of spicated yellow flowers.

Other common species, of "foreign" origin, exist, especially in the center of the chain, such as the Callis-

grassy steppes as one goes northwestward. The eastern Himalayas are conspicuous for the exceptional abundance of species. Although still unprecisely known, it is estimated that there are over 4,000 species of flowering plants, not to mention the numerous varieties of palm trees, bamboo trees and broad-leafed trees.

temon citrinus, whose drooping branches bear clusters of flowers resembling aspergillums and eucalyptus trees (Eucalyptus globus, E. amygdalina), both from Australia, the Jacaranda mimosifolia, with its thousands of tiny violet flowers, imported from Brazil, and the sensitive or American mimosa (Mimosa pudica).

As one ascends the slopes, one finds forests of oaks (Quercus glauca, Q. leucotrichophora, Q. baloot), pines, including the chir pine (Pinus roxburghii) with reddish scales on its trunk, alders (Alnus nepalensis, A. nitida) on the eastern margin of the chain, and olive trees (Olea ferruginea), more prevalent in the west.

While the forests of the western Himalayas are home to xerophilous species, of the acacia family (Albizia julibrissin) or the Persian acacia (A. chinensis, Robinia pseudacacia or false acacia) and of the jujube family (Zizyphus mauritiana), these progressively give way to

The temperate zone

Most parts of the three temperate zones also have extensive forest development, although there are other types of trees as well. One encounters oaks (Quercus lamellosa, Q. lanata, Q. semecarpifolia which are found up to altitudes of 12,400 feet), cedars (Cedrus deodara), maples (Acer oblongum, A. pentapomicum, A. campbellii, A. sterculiaceum), hornbeams (Carpinus viminea, C. faginea), cypresses (Cupressus torulosa, C. corneyana), poplars (Populus caspica, P. ciliata, known as Himalayan poplar, P. nigra, in the western reaches of the chain, P. jacquemontiana, in the east), birches (Betula utilis, B. alnoides), chestnut trees (Castanopsis indica, C. hystrix) and especially great numbers of conifers. Among the latter, one encounters pines (Pinus wallichiana, the famous blue pine of the Himalayas, P. gerardania), firs (Abies spectabilis, nicknamed golden conifer, A. pindrow, which

A mountainside covered with rhododendrons, in spring, in Arunachal Pradesh. These glistening bushes can be over 33 feet high. They grow in acid soil in the temperate alpine belts.

grows in the west and A. *densa*, in the east), larches (*Larix griffithiana*, L. *himalaica*), spruces (*Picea smithiana* in the west, P. *spinulosa* in the east), and yews (*Taxus wallichiana*). Ferns (Aspidium, Sinopterdiaceae, Asplenium), epiphyte lichens (usnea) that hang from the branches of trees and moss (hypnaceae, bryaceae) often in association with lichens, are all plentiful. So are flowering plants, such as ivies (*Hedera nepalensis, Helwingia himalaica, Panax pseudo-gingseng* which can be found up to 14,000 feet, *Aralia cachmirica, Trevesia palmata*), laurels (various species of *Cinnamomum, Dodecadenia, Persea, Linaera, Litsea*), rosaceae, including dog-rose (*Rosa brunonii* or nutmeg rose of the Himalayas, R. *foetida*, R. *webbiana*), hawthorns (*Crataegus songarica*), magnolias (*Magnolia campbelli*, M. *globosa*), viburnums, (*Viburnum grandiflorum*, V. *nervosum*), and bauhinias, with "camel's foot " leaves (*Bauhinia variegata*, B. *purpurea*, B. *vahlii*). Finally, there are those splendid orchids relatively rare below 2,600 feet and often in limited areas, fairly equally distributed among the ground species (*eulophia, calanthe, dactylorhiza, galearis, satyrium, habenaria, pecteilis, ponerorchis, platanthera, malaxis, spathoglottis, oreorchis, spiranthes, galeola, herminium*) and the epiphytal varieties, supported by trees or rocks (*rhynchostylis, vanda, aerides, coelogyne, pleione, bulbophyllum, cymbidium, cryptochilus, dendrobium,vandopsis*). 314 species have been identified in Nepal, 513 in Sikkim and until the present time, 800 in Assam and Arunachal Pradesh. Above 9,100 feet one begins to find rhododendrons (an important variety of the ericaceae family) with over one hundred varieties in the Himalayas and which have become the national trees of Nepal and Bhutan.

In February and March when the first plants bloom until mid-June when the monsoons begin to wreak havoc among the flowers, the countryside is a fabulous splash of colors. Limitless tiers of rhododendrons rise along the slopes, from arborescent forms that may reach heights of 65 feet, whereas their European cousins remain modest bushes, to dwarf varieties that come into view as one reaches the tree line. The nuances are infinite, with the deeper hues (red, purple, violet and mauve) predominating from 8,200 to 10,800 feet. From there on until 13,000 feet, the various tints of pink rise in thick massifs. Further up, the pinks fade progressively turning to yellow and ochre-green and finally give way to white around 14,700 feet.

The alpine zone

The three stages of the alpine zone present relatively homogeneous physiognomies. Between 11,800 and 12,500 feet, the forest progressively gives way to shrubs and bushes, such as junipers (*Juniperus communis*, J. *recurva*, J. *squamata*, J. *indica*, or black juniper used as incense in Buddhist sanctuaries), honeysuckles (*Lonicera rupicola*, L. *purpurascens*, L. *cyanocarpa*, L. *hypoleuca*), and caragana (*Caragana versicolor*, C. *brevifolia*, C. *gerar-*

The Himalayan forests, especialy in the eastern part of the range, contain huge tracts of conifers (pines, firs,cedars, spruces and larches) whose trunks are over 164 feet high. Heavy exploitation is gradually deforesting these mountains.

diana, C. *jubata*) which yield to the artemisia (*Artemisia dracunculus*, A. *wallichiana*, A. *brevifolia*) in the more humid zones.

Above 13,000 feet in dry zones and 14,500 feet in humid zones, there are no trees. The ground, on the other hand, is blanketed with low plants up to the snowline. The lower alpine zone consists of heaths and scrub-covered steppe; the upper alpine zone, of short grass and lawns whose gramineous plants are the basic cover vegetation.

Other species are represented by the Ranunculaceae (numerous species of *Anemone*, *Caltha*, *Trollius*, *Paraquilegia*, *Aquilegia*, *Delphinium*), the Cyperaceae (genus *Scirpus*, *Cyperus*, *Rhynchospora*, *Elyna* and especially the carex or sedge with sharp-edged leaves), the leguminous plants (*Cicer*, *Chesneya*, *Hedysarum*, around forty *Astragalus* and twenty odd similar plants *Oxytropis*), some Cruciferae (*Braya*, *Draba*, *Thlaspi*, *Cardamine*, *Brassica*), Scrophulariaceae (*Scrophularia*, *Lancea*, *Lagotis*, *Oreosolen*, different species of Veronica and the double-lipped *Pedicularis*), Papaveraceae (*Meconopsis*, including the famous blue poppy or *Meconopsis horridula*, *Corydalis*), Gentianaceae (including thirty species of *Swertia*, fifteen *Gentianella* and over sixty *Gentiana* which, in the Himalayas generally have two-toned blue and white alternating petals on the corolla), Asteraceae (*Aster*, *Leontopodium* or edelweiss, *Waldheimia*, *Cremanthodium*, nearly forty species of purple or pink-flowered *Saussurea*, and approximately thirty species of *Senecico* with yellow feather-like flowers), Primulaceae (over twenty plants of the *Androsace* genus and more than fifty species of *Primula*, commonly called primrose, including the *farinosae*, *minutissimae*, *nivales*, *soldanelloides*). Lichens abound and their dense colonizations produce saxicolous vegetation (vicarious species on carbonatite or silica rocks). It is difficult, however, to limit the mosses and lichens to one precise geographic locality. Indeed, because of the volatility of their spores in a windy environment, their colonization corresponds more to a particular biotope (soil, shade, temperature affinities). This is especially true for certain lichens found on granite rocks in the Alps as well as in the Arctic region. Vegetation in the subnivean and nival zones must adapt to the rigor and poverty of this plantless world in which life-sustaining conditions diminish with altitude. This is the home of the Crassulaceae (numerous species of *Rhodiola*, *Sedum* or stonecrop) and the Saxifragaceae, among which the eye-catching saxifrage (*Saxifraga hirculoides*, S. *lychnitis*, S. *saginoides*, S. *pulvinaria*), bergenia (*Bergenia stracheyi*, B *purpurascens*), and the golden saxifrage (*Chrysosplenium carnosum*). Some of these perennials look like cushions and at night restore the heat accumulated during the day. They have one very strong main root that delves deep into the cracks in the rocks. One must not omit some Primulaceae of the *Androsace* genus (*Androsace delavayi*, A. *tapete*, A. *zam-*

balensis) and the *Primula* genus (*Primula minutissima*, P. *reptans*, P. *walshii*).

Last but not least, there are three sub-families of Caryophyllaceae which furnish the highest altitude plants in the world: the campion, the arenaria, and the starwort. Campions (*Silene nigrescens*, S. *gonosperma*) grow at a somewhat lower altitude than the two other

A *branch of* Euphorbia pulcherrima, *originally from Central America very common in the tropics (here Central Nepal). This sturdy thornless tree can grow up to 13 feet in height.*

varieties, the arenaria (*Arenaria polytrichoides*, A. *edgeworthiana*, A. *glanduligera*, and the white-flowered *Arenaria bryophilla* which grows up to an altitude of 20,275 feet), and the white-flowered starwort (the *Stellaria decumbens*, which holds the record according to the "Guiness Book of Records" for growing at an altitude of 20,128 feet, an achievement contested only by the afore-mentioned arenaria).

Above this extends the region of ice where no plant life exists.

In the high meadows from ▶
Uttar Pradesh to Tibet,
between 11,400 and
16,400 feet, one frequently
sees primroses (here
Primula tibetica), near
the torrents. They often
have a blackish calyx.

The grassy land of the ▶▶
Himalayas between 9,800
feet and 14,700 feet
is sometimes dotted with
edelweiss (Leontopodiun
jacotianum). This plant
has bracts and woolen-like
leaves.The little "pompoms"
in the middle are composite
flowers.

In the rocky semi-barren ▶
ground of high altitudes
(between 10,800 and
14,700 feet) one
sometimes sees bright
yellow inflorescences, 6 to
12 inches tall, with large
oblong leaves. They are
Cremanthodium
arnicoides (here in
Dolpo).

A beautiful specimen of ▶▶
Aster Strachevi found in
Himachal Pradesh. They
can be found as far as
eastern Bhutan between
11,500 and 14,800 feet.
The different species of this
perennial plant are of
various shades of lilac
and have very few leaves.

The elephant (Elephas maximus) *is inseparable from the image of India.*
Its smaller ears and size distinguish it from its African cousin.
Nevertheless, it can weigh four to five tons.

The fauna of the Himalayas is as rich as the flora on which it is closely dependent. Certain very rare animals, unfortunately, are threatened with extinction. The distribution of animal life is related to the climate which governs the means of subsistence required by each species. Traditionally, there are three important zones inhabited by animals: the lowlands, the mountains, and the high mountains. As with the flora, it is impossible to present an exhaustive account of all the Himalayan species. The predominance of certain species in each zone has determined our choice.

The lowlands

The tropical forests, and more generally the hot, humid lowlands below 5,000 feet, are essentially the home of reptiles and large mammals. Among the latter the most important are the elephant (*Elephas maximus*) and two endangered species which, although they are now protected, are becoming extinct: the great Indian rhinoceros (*Rhinoceros unicornis*) and the tiger (*Panthera tigris*). Until India became independent in 1947, they were the favorite prey of hunters. King George V and his suite alone killed thirty-nine tigers in eleven days during the winter of 1911-1912. From 1938 to 1940 the King of Nepal's guests slaughtered four hundred thirty-three tigers and fifty-three rhinoceroses in the Terai jungle. It is estimated that only one hundred and fifty tigers remain today and fewer than two hundred and fifty one-horned rhinoceroses. In the trees, the panther (*Panthera nebulosa*) mainly hunts monkeys which abound in the region as do langurs and hanumans (*Presbytis entellus*) with their dark faces and legs, golden monkeys (*Rhinopithecus roxellanae*), a very rare species only found in the far eastern Himalayas, the rhesus (*Macaca mulatta*, *M. assamensis*) with its red-brown fur and pink face, as well as various species of gibbons (*Hylobates hoolock*).

Many bovidae also live in the lower belt. Most abundant of these are the zebu (*Bos indicus*), the Indian buffalo or water buffalo (*Bubalus bubalis*), which alone constitutes half of the livestock and is widely used for work in the fields, the wide-browed, short-horned gayal (*Bos frontalis*), the enormous wild ox (*Bos gaurus*), most prevalent in the west, the nilgaut or bluebull (*Boselaphus tragocamelus*), one of India's most beautiful ruminants, the black antelope (*Antilopa cervicapra*), which lives at the edges of forests, and the four-horned antelope (*Tetraceros quadricornis*) (only the males have this feature which is unique among the bovidae). There are also cervidae, such as the muntjak or barking deer (*Muntiacus muntjak*), the barasingha or swamp deer (*Cervus duvauceli*), the Thorold deer (*Cervus albirostris*), the chital or axis deer (*Axis axis*), and the pig deer (*Axis porcinus*). One should not fail to mention the mongoose (*Herpestes edwardsi* or grey mongoose, H. *auropunctatus*) and countless rodents.

The fauna

Reptiles exist in great numbers, although limited to only a few species. The most frequently encountered are the thin-snouted gharial (*Gavialis gangeticus*), the generally harmless crocodile (*Crocodylus palustris*), various water turtles (of the *Emys*, *Amyda* and *Platysternum* genera), land turtles (of the *Testude* genus), geckos (of the *gymnodactylus* and *phyllodactylus* genera, including the 13 3/4 inches long gecko *verticillatus*, the giant of the family), skinks (of the *Ristella* genus) and numerous lizards (among which the Agamidae of the *phrynocephalus* genus which are oviparous at low altitudes and viviparous at 4,500 feet). Serpents are represented by Colubridae, such as the Indian ratter (*Ptyas mucosus*), the "egg-eater" (*Elachistodon westermanni*), Boidae among which the bi-colored python (*Python molurus*) that may reach a length of 23 feet, Viperidae (*Vipera russelli*) and the Elapidae which are the most dangerous of the venomous snakes, including the Indian cobra (*Naja naja*) and the deadly royal cobra (*Ophiophagus hannah*), which can attain a length of 20 feet.

There are also amphibians (of the *Bufo*, *Rana*, *Salamandra* and *Triturus* genera), mollusks (of the *Hellix* and *Limax* genera) and earthworms (especially Oligochaeta and leeches). Many of these same animals can be found with various adaptations at upper stages, such as the black toad (*Bufo malanosticus*) or the green toad (*Bufo viridis*) that live at elevations of up to 15,500 feet. In certain rivers of the Terai and Arunachal Pradesh, one can even find that remarkable mammal, the fresh-water dolphin (*Platanista gangetica*).

The Himalayas are not particularly rich in fish. There is, however, an unusual species, the *sahar* (*Barbus tor*) that makes its way from its distant ocean home to spawn in the mountain torrents.

Birds, on the other hand, are omnipresent. There are the antigone crane (*Grus antigone*), the yellow-beaked pirol (*Urocissa flavirostris*), the pagoda starling (*Sturnus pagodarum*), the red waxbill (*Estrilda amandava*), the manyar weaver (*Ploceus manyar*), the red sparrow (*Passer rutilans*), and the blue peacock (*Pavo cristatus*), *Gallus sonnerati*, etc. So far, no fewer than 1,200 species have been identified in all the climatic stages of the entire Himalayan area. Extensive research has yet to be conducted in Arunachal Pradesh and southeast Tibet.

The middle mountains

The montane zone covers the temperate stages and stops at the lower alpine zone. Fish are relatively scarce in the numerous rivers, although the wild waters harbor various species of trout (of the *Salmo* genus). On the other hand, birds and bovidae are plentiful. The list of birds seems interminable, there are so many different species. The yellow-beaked chough is frequently seen (*Pyrrhocorax graculus*), even as high as 27,330 feet as it eats the left-overs of an expedition, the blue magpie (*Ciffa occipitalis*), the striped hoopoe

(*Upupa epops longirostris*), the blue red-breast (*Erithacus brunneus*), the bar-headed goose (*Anser indicus*), the snow grouse (*Tetrogallus thibetanus*), the black-necked crane (*Grus nigricollis*), the horned lark (*Eremophyla alpestris*), the Shimla black tit (*Parus ater*), the blue nightingale (*Grandala coelicolor*), the nut-cracker (*Nucifraga caryocatactes*), the accentor (*Prunella collaris*, *P. modularis*), the snow pigeon (*Columba leuconota*), the snow finch (*Montifringilla nivalis*), the Hodgson finch (*Fringilla hodgsoni*), the Nepal sunbird (*Aethopyga nepalensis*), and one must not forget the magnificent shining monal pheasant (*Lophophorus impejanus*). This bronze-feathered member of the Phasiandae has a crest resembling that of the peacock and only lives above 11,500 feet. It has become the national bird of Nepal.

Among the mammals, one finds cervidae including the Kashmir stag (a sub-species of *Axis*), the sambar (*Cervus unicolor*), and occasionally, according to peasants, a shou or Sikkim stag, which is considered to be extinct. One commonly comes across marmots (*Marmota himalayana*, *M. bobak*), shrews (*Tupaia glis*, *Anathana ellioti*), porcupines (*Hystrix cristata*), hedgehogs (*Paraechinus micropus*, *Hemiechinus auritus*), squirrels (*Dremonys lokriah*), ratels, (*Mellivora capensis*), foxes (*Vulpes ferrilata*), otters (*Lutra perspicillata*), weasels (*Mustela altaica*), and yellow-bellied martens (*Martes flavigula*). Wolves (*Canis lupus*) predominate in the upper regions, as do the dangerous wild dogs or dhole (*Cuon alpinus*) who hunt in packs at 13,000 feet, the kiang or wild ass (*Equus hemionus kiang*) with its white rump, feet and muzzle, the mottled cat (*Felis marmorata*), the red panda (*Ailurus fulgens*), a lovely little carnivore that lives at heights between 9,800 and 13,000 feet, and bears. One finds the brown bear (*Ursus isabellinus*) and the black bear (*Selenarctos thibetanus*) with a white patch under its neck. It is the most dangerous animal of the Himalayas.

But the Caprineae are the most common of the ruminants, the Himalayas being home to the greatest number of species in the world. Among the bovines one finds the Tibetan ox (*Bos taurus*), the many varieties of the *zo* (a hybrid between the zebu or the Tibetan ox and a yak), perfectly adapted for high-altitude work, the yak (*Bos grunniens*) and the *drong* (a massive yak living above 16,000 feet elevation). The two most common species of antelope are the *chiru* or Tibetan antelope (*Pantholops hodgsoni*) and the Himalayan gazelle (*Gazella procapra picticaudata*). The Caprineae are represented by the takin (*Budorcas taxicolor*), whose thick fleece gives it the false appearance of a yak, the ruffled mufflon (*Ammotragus lervia*), the bharal (*Pseudois nayaur*), the Himalayan tahr (*Hemitragus jemlahicus*), the serow (*Capricornus sumatrensis*), the goral chamois (*Naemorhedusgoral*) and the musk deer (*Moschus moschiferus*), a particularly endangered species since 40,000 of them were slaughtered to make perfumes and various medicines. There are large groups of goats and sheep. In

addition to the common goat (*Capra hircus*) some of whose members (in the Karakorum, Kashmir and Changthang) have "angora" wool, there are the ibex (*Capra ibex sibirica*), which lives in the far western reaches of the Himalayas, the wild goat (*Capra aegagrus*), and the markhor (*Capra falconeri*), both of which are endangered species. In the sheep family one finds

the common sheep (*Ovis aries*), the shapo or wild sheep (*Ovis vignii*), the argali (*Ovis ammon hodgsoni*) and the urial (*Ovis ammon orientalis*), a sub-species of the argali.

The high mountains

The high mountain belt goes from the upper alpine zone to the limit of the inorganic world. These are the preferred grounds of certain rare mammals, a few big birds and a multitude of insects. The most famous, rarely seen, mammal is the magnificent snow panther (*Panthera uncia*), commonly called ounce, with its white coat and dark spots. The birds are the bearded vulture (*Gypaetus barbatus*) whose wing spread may reach 9 feet, the eagle (*Ictinactus malayensis*), and the griffon vulture (*Gyps fulvus himalayensis*), all birds of prey or feeding on carrion.

Insects seem to be the animals best adapted to this hostile environment. There are Orthoptera (grasshoppers and crickets), Hymenoptera (bees and bumblebees), Arachnida (spiders of the *Salticus* genus) that along with the Coleoptera (of the *Carabus* genus) feed on mini-arthropoda, and especially the Lepidoptera.

A tiger (Panthera tigris) *from Terai. For many years the reputation of this splendid feline proved almost fatal to it. Hunters massacred thousands of animals just to have prestigious trophies. The current protective policy may allow the last representatives of the species to be saved.*

There are, indeed, a great variety of moths and butter-flies, in fact, thousands of species. The former are mainly noctua (of the Noctuid family), phalaena (of the geometridae family), bombyx and sphinx, or hawk-moths (of the notodontidae and sphingidae families). Among the most beautiful are the sulphurs (genus, *Colias* and *Pieris*), the nymphals (genus *Boloria* and *Euphydryas*), and the satyr butterflies (genus *Coeno-nympha* and *Erebia*), the Papilionidae (particularly the *Parnassius* genus). They fly up to altitudes of 18,000 feet and feed on the subsisting plants, saxifrages for the parnassius, gramineous plants for the Erebia. As summer is so short, it takes them two years to deve-lop completely. Thus, the caterpillar hibernates twice.

The langur (Presbytis entellus) *are abundant in the lowlands. They are arboreal, leaf-eating monkeys. Their dark faces contrast with their light fur. These relatively timorous animals are unfortunately often victims of hunters.*

Two marmots (Marmota himalayana) *from Zanskar coming out of their burrow in the beginning of spring after hibernating. This is when, eager for food, they are most exposed to various predators.*

The colors and the multitude of shapes are a delight to the eyes. Two in particular, deserve special mention: the snowy-white *Parnassius imperator*, whose rear wings have two beautiful pairs of bright red eyes, and three pairs of smaller black eyes with blue pupils, and finally, the *Bhutanitis lidderdalei* with blackish-brown striped front wings and delicatedly caudated dark red and black-spotted rear wings.

◄◄ *The enormous griffon vulture* (Gyps fulvus himalayanus) *feeds on carrion and haunts the barren mid-heights. It is much bigger than its European cousin. Its wingspread can attain 9 feet and its weight is from 25.5 to 33 pounds.*

◄ *The three-meter-long snake is a magnificent example of the royal cobra* (Ophiophagus hannah). *This fearsome specimen was caught in Kameng, in Arunachal Pradesh, then sold to itinerant tumblers who exhibit it for a few rupees as they travel along their way.*

◄◄ *There are many varieties of Cervidae in the Himalayas. Among them the muntjak* (Muntiacus muntjak) *which lives in temperate zones at the upper limit of the lowlands . It is found in southeast Asia as far as the Sunda Islands.*

◄ *The resplendent lophophore* (Lophophorus impejanus) *is a magnificent Phasianidae with lustrous bronze feathers. It lives between 6,500 feet and 16,400 feet in open oak and coniferous forests. Its rarity and beauty have made it the national bird of Nepal.*

The yak (Bos grunniens) *is* ►
remarkably well adapted to high altitudes, which makes it is a much sought after pack animal. This adult specimen was photographed at the beginning of winter in central Bhutan. One can only imagine the size of the rhododendrons around it.

Greco-Buddhist vestiges of the Gandhara empire are plentiful
in the low valleys of the north, where the civilization spread from its capitals
Taxila and Purushpura, situated in the southern plains.

Ancient Times

The Himalayas have been the subject of literature and popular rumors for over three thousand years. The Chinese, Tibetans and Indians mentioned the giant mountains in many of their religious and mythological texts, and their legendary heroes' exploits often took place there. But the enchanted realm of the gods really only entered history in the middle of the sixth century BC when the independent kingdom of Gandhara was founded in the northwest of what is now Pakistan. Once it became a province of the great contemporary Persian empire it developed a remarkable culture, heavily permeated by primitive Indian Buddhism. Two centuries later, Gandhara was conquered by Alexander the Great's soldiers to whom the powerful Persians had succumbed. The region then came under the influence of the Scythians and the Parthians. During the first century of the Christian era, the Kushans of Afghanistan led by King Kanishka established a formidable empire stretching from the Aral Sea to the Ganges and from Baluchistan to the Pamirs and Tibet. Under their protection, Buddhism continued to spread and Gandhara became the center of the greatest art school of the times, harmoniously blending Greek canons and Buddhist themes. In the third century the weakening of the Kushan empire proved advantageous to new conquerors, especially the Sassanids who annexed Gandhara and did not hesitate to intervene politically and militarily in the regions to the east, bringing aid, for example, to Patola Shahi, a dynasty of sovereigns who succeeded in uniting under their banner most of the tribes of the upper Indus and the Gilgit Rivers. In return, the foreign protectors obtained the right of inspection over Bolor (known as Dardistan in the 8th century) and could oversee the Tarim basin, the important crossroad on the Silk Route.

The emergence of the great Himalayan powers

In the central Himalayas one country emerged from legendary mists to enter the history of the third century of the Christian era: Nepal. The Kiratas or Kirantis (whose name means "savages" or "mountain people"), a small tribe that arrived from the east at the end of the first century BC mounted the throne. Under their rule, Buddhism, which had been imported by Indian monks, spread along the major valleys. The Licchavi dynasty succeeded the Kiratas at the end of the 5th century and their most illustrious king, Amshuvarman, married his daughter Bhrikuti to the Tibetan king, Songtsen Gampo, in 641.

At this point in history Tibet was merely a gathering of seventeen disparate fiefs united by King Namri around the principality of Yarlung, not far from Lhasa. The early Tibetans known by the name of Kiang had

The history of men

long been written of in Chinese chronicles which mention the presence in the mountains south of Kukunor of dangerous nomadic barbarians and distinguished horsemen that general Chao Chong Ko had great difficulty in beating off in 62 BC. Twenty years later the same Kiangs again attacked the Chinese positions. Only the massive intervention of general Fong Fong Che was able to drive them away towards Tsaidam. At the end of the 4th century the Tibetans were again heard of because of their unceasing incursions into Chinese territory. The Chinese sovereigns avoided confronting them directly, preferring to use diplomacy to direct their movements towards neighboring countries.

At the death of King Namri, his son Songtsen Gampo continued his work; through force or alliances he united various fiefs, chieftainries and principalities. Influenced by his two wives, both of whom were fervent Buddhists, the Nepalese Bhrikuti and the Chinese Wengcheng, daughter of the emperor of China Tai Zong (the first sovereign of the Tang dynasty) whom he also married in 641, Songtsen Gampo adopted Buddhism as the official religion. Both queens, moreover, appear in religious iconography respectively as the "Green Tara" and the "White Tara".

Meanwhile, China had become a great regional power. It possessed a remarkable administration and a well-trained army. When the Tang dynasty came to power in 618 it opted for an armed peace with its southern neighbors, Tibet and Nepal. The latter, under Kings Thakuri and Malia, took advantage of the situation to reinforce its authority and consolidate its independence. The Hindu-Buddhist religious system which is so special in Nepal, was codified at that time and the caste system founded. Tibetan living conditions improved as a result of frequent contacts with China and especially India, whose culture was then flourishing throughout the entire sub-continent.

The Tibetan hegemony

However, the rise to power of Tibet, which was considered an Indian outpost, worried the Chinese. Between 659 and 714, events moved fast. As relations with China worsened, the Tibetans conquered Kukunor, eastern Turkestan (which the Chinese took back in 692), and concluded military alliances with the Turks against the Chinese. War soon broke out. First the Tibetans won, but then they suffered three successive defeats in 714, 725 and 727.

En 730 both countries signed a peace treaty, despite which the Tibetans continued to raid the Chinese entrepôts, provoking reprisals by the Tang emperors, whose soldiers and merchants had spread to the far corners of the Himalayas, annexing Dardistan and the eastern principalities of Tibet.

In 795, however, King Trisong Detsen mounted the throne in Lhasa. He was a remarkable strategist and a subtle diplomat. He gathered the best army in Asia and entered into alliances with the Turks and the Arabs, both enemies of China. Tibetan power remained at its apogee for two centuries. Its armies were everywhere. To the southwest they invaded Dardistan, drove out the Chinese and subjugated all the small neighboring kingdoms. To the south, they annexed

The Mongol period

The central power, however, was gradually weakened by rivalries among the Tibetan princes and the antagonism between the Buddhist clergy and the *bonpo* priests who had the artistocracy's support. The silent struggle ended with the assassination of the Buddhist King Ralpachen in 838. His brother Langdar-

Ladakh and Baltistan which at the time belonged to Ladakh. To the north, they attacked the main Chinese positions, Samarkand, Khotan, Karachahr, Hami, Shibucheng and even entered Chang'an, the capital of China, which they occupied for several days. To the southeast, Sikkim and Bhutan were victims of constant invasions. Aristocratic Tibetan families settled there at the head of their troops and sliced off sizeable kingdoms for themselves. Only Nepal managed to rebuff the Tibetan onslaught, thanks to the determination of its mountain tribes. For two centuries Tibet remained the master of most of the Himalayas, holding off the Chinese to the north and ensuring the neutrality of the Indian kingdoms to the south.

ma succeeded him. An adept of *Bonpo*, he led a terrible persecution of the Buddhists, until, four years later, he was killed by a monk. What followed was an interminable war of succession during which the country fell into the hands of ministers and heads of religious sects. Tibet faded into obscurity.

The Tibetan Empire was then stripped of its former possessions. The southwest Himalayas passed under the domination of Muslims who had already been present in Chitral since the 10th century and against whom the Tibetans had no recourse. Nor were they capable of resisting the power of Genghis Khan, the new Chinese force that took over from the Song emperors. The great conqueror was recognized as

The region located between Gilgit and Skardu is crisscrossed by trails and roads rich in history. There are a great many sculptures and rupestrian engravings, as well as various writings and inscriptions which reveal the passage of cultures as varied as the Persians, the Parthians, or the Kushans.

supreme leader by the Mongol clans in 1206. He entered Beijing triumphantly five years later. At first, relations between the Mongols and the Tibetans were excellent. Important trade and political relations were established, but Tibet no longer possessed its former military strength. It soon had to accept the Mongol protectorate and pay tribute to Genghis Khan. The Tibetan population rebelled against the new masters and the Mongol armies intervened on several occasions, causing considerable losses. However, they rapidly withdrew from the country each time. The explanation seems to lie in the fear the religious Tibetans inspired in the Mongols who were converting to Buddhism after contact with them. After the death of Genghis Khan, his grandson, Kubilay Khan, reinforced the Sino-Mongol empire by founding the Yuan dynasty. He entertained special relations with the Tibetans and the head of the Sakya monastery, Pandita, became his mentor. Thereafter, Mongol protection would never be lacking. Strengthened by this support, a powerful theocracy was founded in Lhasa. It would soon be dominated by the Dalai Lama ("Ocean" of Wisdom) who, in 1578, was to name another Mongol sovereign, Altan Khan. This same theocracy would rule Tibet until 1959.

Meanwhile, in the forgotten provinces of the western Himalayas, Islam was advancing with lightning speed. In less than a century, all the high valleys of modern Pakistan, Baltistan and the greater part of Kashmir, were converted to the Muslim faith, thus constituting a dangerous threat on the flank of the Mongol empire, which already had begun to decline. Without sufficient means to react, they ultimately abandoned these regions to the Muslim invaders who were arriving from the west in successive waves at the end of the 16th century. Among them could be found the Moghuls, of Turko-Afghan origin, who were to build the most powerful empire on the Indian continent, which they would dominate for approximately two centuries, and which reached from central Afghanistan to Burma and from northern Pakistan to Karnataka in central India.

In Lhasa, politico-religious rivalries increased. The fifth Dalai Lama, Ngawang Lotsang Gyatso, who constructed the Potala, made a final attempt to reunify Tibet. The moribund Yuan dynasty was unable to help, but other Mongols, the Koshot, came to his rescue. Once Tibet was united, these powerful protectors became accustomed to intervening increasingly often in state business. Only the strong personality of Ngawang Lotsang Gyatso restrained them. Before his death in 1682 he handed over all powers to the regent, Tsangyang Gyatso. This skillful politician succeeded in the almost impossible feat of keeping the death of the Dalai Lama secret for fifteen years, in order to preserve the fragile neutrality between the

Mongols and Kang Xi, the Chinese emperor who had mounted the throne in 1662 and who was a member of the Qing Manchu dynasty. A serious incident was to destroy all his efforts. In 1705 a Koshot leader, Lhajang Khan, invaded Tibet, forced his way into Lhasa and killed the regent. The following year, he deposed the sixth Dalai Lama, who was judged too meek, and enthroned a lama of his choice. Another Mongol clan, the Dzungars, then intervened, entering Tibet, which they sacked and pillaged, and killed the Koshot Khan.

Chinese imperialism

This was too good an opportunity for Emperor Kang Xi to ignore, and using the incident as an excuse, he sent his armies into Tibet. The first military expedition resulted in a partial failure because of the Mongol support. A short time later, however, he carried off a splendid victory over the Mongol tribes, which made it possible for him to impose his protectorate over all of Mongolia. He then sent a second expeditionary corps to Tibet. The imperial armies entered Lhasa in 1720. They drove out the Dalai Lama imposed by the Koshots and replaced him by the legitimate pretender, who was immediately enthroned as the seventh Dalai Lama. He was, however, obliged to accept the protection of two Chinese high commissioners who were to control Tibetan policy, as would their successors. In spite of this, the country was again torn between rival selfishness and aristocratic ambitions. Anoble, Pholhanas, was the victorious winner of the ensuing civil war. With Chinese help he became the sovereign of Tibet and for twenty years thereafter the country remained at peace.

But, at his death in 1747, Tibet once again plunged into civil strife that the Dalai Lama was unable to suppress. The revolt of some Tibetans against the Chinese in 1751 opened the door to intervention by imperial troops. Beijing emphasized its annexation of the country after 1757 by allowing the Dalai Lama to retain only spiritual power. China began to look with interest beyond the southern Tibetan border towards the powerful Indian kingdom that a strong sovereign, Prithvi Narayan Shah, had begun to unite.

The European intrusion

Some Europeans, especially members of the powerful British East India Company, had been present in the Indian subcontinent since the beginning of the 17th century. They had first settled in Bihar and Bengal, then had turned towards the mountain regions which bordered them on the north, and had sent out observers. They, however, were not the first Europeans to penetrate into the Himalayas. Others had preceeded them: Jesuits and then Capuchin friars. As early as 1624 two Portugese, Fathers Marques and De Andrada,

had succeeded in crossing the mountain barrier from India and entered Tibet, where they received a warm welcome. They were even allowed to found a mission at Tsaparang. In 1627, the French missionaries, La Cella and Cabral, visited western Bhutan. In 1661, Father Grueber, an Austrian, and Father D'Orville, a Belgian, stopped in the holy city of Lhasa and tried to understand the fundamental elements of Buddhism, in order to oppose it more effectively. Their reports were hardly more encouraging than those of the various Christian missionaries who succeeded one another in the Himalayas for a century. With blatant insincerity, most of these "soul searchers", although competing with each other, agreed in describing a country they did not understand as "an awful region, always covered with snow... and whose local populations have wild and pagan mores that estrange them from the true God". Their observation, however, gave precious information about these little known regions. The first serious map of the Himalayas was drawn up in 1717 by Father Régis from the notes and sketches of two monks sent to Tibet by one of the Chinese emperor's sons. Overly zealous proselytizing, however, disturbed the Buddhist clergy. The attitude of the Christians, who behaved more like spies than clergymen, had become so arrogant that in 1740 King Pholhanas, following repeated complaints from the lamas, closed the only church in Lhasa, constructed in 1725 by the Capuchin friar Della Penna. As a result, in the middle of the 18th century, Tibet and it allies (the kingdoms of Ladakh, Sikkim and Bhutan) totally forbade the presence of foreigners.

Still, the English were more than ever interested in Tibet. They realized that China was master of the situation. Meanwhile, the East Indian Company, with the help of the Crown's soldiers, was able to crush the Moghul power. The Indians, belatedly aware of the danger the European penetration represented, attempted to resist. But by 1756, it was already too late. The principalities fell, one after the other. In 1773, London published the Regulating Act, which

The Potola in Lhasa, the capital of Tibet, was built in the 17th century under the reign of Ngawang Lotsang Gyatso, the fifth Dalai Lama. This palace with more than a thousand rooms remained the official home of the Dalai Lama and the high dignitaries of the Buddhist clergy until 1959 when the Chinese Communist government took over.

unified the English possessions, thus setting the foundations for what would become the British Empire in India and which, a century later, would control the immense territory from eastern Afghanistan to the Sino-Burmese border.

London subsequently set its sights on the Himalayas. This was a time when their mystery and danger

gold and the destruction of Buddhism. Mutilations, torture and executions awaited those Tibetans who gave the slightest assistance to a foreigner.

Suddenly the already strained relations between the British and the countries of the Tibetan region became even more tense. After awkward interventions by British troops in Nepal in 1767 (which ended

Khyber pass is situated in the middle of the Sulaiman hills at the foot of the eastern side of the Hindu Kush range. It is through this natural gateway that over the centuries invaders from the west entered the Indian subcontinent and the Himalayen piedmont.

attracted adventurers. Fifteen odd official missions and an occasional private enterprise brought into these mountains courageous men, many of whom were never to return. The most well-known are Van de Putte, a Dutchman who left Nepal, crossed the Himalayas near Everest and reached Lhasa, and also Bogle, Turner, Manning and Moorcroft who were British. Bogle, who was sent by the East India Company to meet the Panchen Lama in Shigatse, reconnoitered the great trans-Himalayan eastern route that crosses Bhutan; he is said to have married a Tibetan princess. Turner led the first official English mission to Tibet and was the first Westerner to gain entrance into a great monastery. Manning, a rich eccentric, reached Lhasa after an incredibly long journey. Moorcroft, a simple clerk for the East India Company, entered western Tibet via the great western route through Kashmir and by dint of great cunning, obtained the trade monopoly for his company. Contacts between these Westerners and the Tibetans were generally difficult, because official propaganda, fostered by China, described all foreigners as lowly adventurers exclusively interested in

in a bitter defeat for the English at the battle of Sindhuli), in Bhutan and Sikkim between 1773 and 1776, and under pressure from the Dalai Lama, these countries, as well as Ladakh, Zanskar and Spiti thereafter forbade access to their mountains to all Westerners. As a result, by the end of the 18th century, the Himalayas had become a forbidden region.

For a period of fifteen years the Nepalese sovereigns bent their efforts towards consolidating their realms, while keeping an eye on the English. Yet it was from the north that the danger was to come. Quite suddenly, the Dalai Lama, manipulated by Chinese diplomacy, sent his troops to invade the kingdom. The Tibetans approached Kathmandu, but Bahadur Shah, Prithvi Narayan's grandson, succeeded in holding them back. In addition, he took up the offensive and entered Tibet, where he seized the city of Shigatse and the wealthy monastery of Tashilhunpo. The Chinese emperor, who had been warned of the threat, proceeded to attack the Nepalese directly, and brilliantly repelled them. The Treaty of Betravati in 1792 ended hostilities without designating vanquished or vanquisher, but it allowed the Chinese to permanently impose their suzerainty on Tibet, thereafter considered a mere southern province of the empire. Only the western (Ladakh, Spiti, Lahul) and eastern (Sikkim, Bhutan, Towang) regions managed to retain relative autonomy.

The English, however, did not stop there. Their ultimate objective was Tibet, the key to the Himalayas. Cautiously, they first sent out scouts, the famous pandits, those pilgrim-spy-cartographers, who went out disguised as peaceful monks and hermits, to gather a maximum amount of strategic information by wandering along the trans-Himalayan roads, from Hunza to Ladakh, and from Bhutan to Tibet. Then, armed with this precious knowledge they militarily attacked the front line of countries. Nepal was the first, in 1814. Two years later it was forced to sign the treaty of Sagauli, in which London obliged King Bahadur Shah to accept the presence of a permanent Resident in Kathmandu, a sort of first Western ambassador in the forbidden valley. That was the extent of the only English intrusion into Nepal, which was able to conserve its independence until the British departure from India in 1947.

Shortly thereafter, Sikkim, Bhutan and Ladakh were defeated and had to accept English protectorates. The road to Tibet was now open.

Anglo-Russian rivalry

Meanwhile, another empire had appeared in central Asia, the empire of the Russian Czars, whose growing power worried the English. For decades, spies from both countries had been crossing paths in the Tibetan region. In 1865 the English, thanks to their pandits, began secretly to draw up detailed maps of Tibet. In 1872, a Russian colonel, Nicolas Przewalski, entered northern Tibet with a small escort of Cossacks, and collected much geographical and political information.

The rivalry between the British and Russian empires grew as incidents between them occurred. New clergymen came to Tibet, repeating the same errors as their predecessors. The French Lazarist Fathers Huc and Gabet arrived in Lhasa from China in 1846, left after riots broke out and were the cause of further diplomatic complications among France, Russia and England. The eleventh Dalai Lama, Khedrup Gyatso, took advantage of the situation to close Tibet once again. The attitudes of the sovereigns of Ladakh, Sikkim and Bhutan became more rigid in response to requests by the authorities in Lhasa as well as the benevolent complicity of the English who were intent on keeping the Himalayas for themselves. Frictions between Tibet and Nepal, "protected" by England, degenerated into a war from 1854 to 1856. The Czar Alexander II signed a treaty of friendship with the Tibetans which granted the Russians important trade and strategic privileges and which the English considered inimical to their interests.

The combination of these events convinced the English to intervene, first, through diplomatic channels with the aid of the French. From Beijing, they tried to counter the Russian influence; then they reinforced their military positions in the western Himalayas by forming a large regional federation of the majority of the small Muslim kingdoms of northern Pakistan and Kashmir devoted to their cause, and in the east by accentuating their control over Sikkim, Bhutan and Assam.

In 1903, as a result of unfounded rumors that China had granted the Russians advantages in Tibet, including important mining concessions, England decided to launch a military effort against Lhasa. Colonel Younghusband's expedition entered the city the following year, after having forced its way through the Tibetan army, which lost hundreds of men in the operation. The conqueror imposed on the regent (who had replaced the 13th Dalai Lama, Thupten Gyatso, who had fled to Mongolia) a treaty granting economic and political privileges exclusively to the British.

Two treaties were to complete the British project. In 1906, London signed The Peking Convention with China, in which it recognized Chinese suzerainty over Tibet, and obtained in exchange economic control of Tibet. In 1907, London signed a non-aggression treaty with Russia, guaranteeing the security of the Himalayan borders.

Pax Britannica ruled the entire Himalayas.

Modern times

The Manchu dynasty, prey to serious difficulties, considered reestablishing its prestige by annexing Tibet, where the 13th Dalai Lama was ruling after his return from Mongolia. They were encouraged by the Western powers and Russia who hardly appreciated the British monopoly in the region. In 1910 Chinese troops intervened brutally in eastern Tibet. The Tibetans revolted immediately and the Dalai Lama fled to India where he was under English protection. However, there was a sudden change in the Chinese situation; the Manchu dynasty was overthrown and the newly-founded republic quickly confirmed its ambitions in Tibet. Confrontations with the Tibetans, united around the Dalai Lama, once again in India, increased. British diplomats brought the adversaries together for negotiations in Shimla in 1913-1914. The ensuing convention which recognized almost total autonomy for Tibet was not ratified by China. The three nations, however, reached an agreement, even though China did not officially ratify the famous MacMahon line, a border that ran from Ladakh to Assam. Behind the scenes the English tried to cut Tibet off from all other influences. This was the aim of the 1920-1921 mission of Sir

Charles Bell, who converted to Buddhism and became the Dalai Lama's counselor. Despite these efforts, relations between the two countries deteriorated.

In Nepal, the Ranas had been ruling since 1846, when a powerful minister from this clan took the royal family under its wing. A remarkable statesman, Jung Bahadur directed all his efforts to maintaining the

rate state and were encouraged by India. Kashmir also brought the Indo-Pakistani antagonisms to a head. The Hindu sovereign of this large Muslim state decided to join the Indian Union, thus starting the first war between Pakistan and India. The 1949 armistice set up a demarcation line between the belligerents, but Delhi retained control of three-quarters of Kashmir.

The Rampur palace with its very "kitsch" architecture, has been modified several times. It belongs to the maharaja of Pattiala, a descendant of the prestigious dynasty of the Bushen (or Busher) sovereigns who dominated the whole history of the central Pradesh Himalayas.

realm's independence against its powerful neighbors and to increasing contacts with the rest of the world. He was received both in Paris and in London. He successfully protected his country from the upheavals sweeping through the Himalayas and even managed to repulse British protection which was spreading over the whole Indian sub-continent. Above all, he avoided getting involved in the regional conflicts. His successors, pursuing the same policy, consolidated the independence of Nepal which was to be the only Himalayan country not to have suffered foreign domination.

And yet, two major events were to upset the fragile balance in the region: the independence of India and the birth of the People's Republic of China.

In 1947, India won its independence from England, but the nation was divided into two district states owing to ancestral religious rivalries between Muslims and Hindus. India's majority is Hindu, whereas the Muslims obtained Pakistan, which was composed of two separate part 1,100 miles apart: western Pakistan northwest of India, and eastern Pakistan, in the northeast. The people of eastern Pakistan, ethnically quite distinct from the Indo-Europeans of western Pakistan, immediately demonstrated their wish to have a sepa-

In 1951 the Nepalese regime of the Ranas fell after a popular uprising provoked from Delhi by King Tribhuvan, the grandfather of the current monarch. Once he returned to Kathmandu, Tribhuvan restored the royal dynasty after an exemplary revolution without any bloodshed.

Things went less well in Tibet. In 1949, Mao Zedong proclaimed the People's Republic of China. The Chinese military presence in Lhasa which had been fairly modest was considerably increased, causing new uprisings. In 1951, invoking the principle of the liberation of oppressed peoples and normalization, Chinese soldiers annexed Tibet. The feudal tradition and the theocratic system were the two main targets of the Communists. The repression was particularly violent. In 1959, Tenzing Gyatso, the present Dalai Lama, had to flee to India, where he continues to live.

Three nuclear powers on the Roof of the World

The Himalayas now comprise three major regional powers: Pakistan, India and China. All three have expansionist objectives which have rapidly become manifest and which require an enormous arsenal. The equally obvious place for this confrontation is the Himalayas. It is here in the peaceful highlands of the Roof of the World that fighting is likely to break out. A war already took place between India and China in 1962. Troops from Beijing invaded Aksai Chin (the eastern part of Ladakh, claimed by China) and all of the northern part of the N.E.F.A. (North East Frontier

Most of the north Indian maharajas (here the maharaja of Gvalior, a city quite distant from the Himalayas) were interested in the mountains. They provided troops to the English colonizer in order to conquer the mythical mountains.

Agency), the former name of Arunachal Pradesh. The Indian army was brushed away. Nevertheless, the Chinese retreated, satisfied at having proven their military superiority, although they kept control of Aksai Chin. India, which was humiliated by the defeat, launched an enormous war effort with Soviet aid. Pakistan and China did the same and became reconciled. Although the former was a member of the Western camp, and the latter belonged to the Communist bloc, they have always maintained good relations. India and Pakistan accepted the principle that Kashmir should be divided, but were incapable of agreeing on a demarcation line. In 1965, taking advantage of the revolt among the Muslim communities in India, Pakistan started a new war. The Indian army, with its greater numbers, was able to repel the attack and enter Pakistani territory. Then China caused disturbances on the Sikkim border in order to aid its ally. International public opinion and the Sikkim threat were instrumental in bringing Delhi to sign a ceasefire, which was confirmed in 1966 at the Peace Conference in Tashkent.

In 1971, hostilities broke out again between Pakistan and India, this time over eastern Pakistan, with Delhi giving its support to the autonomist move-

ments. Pakistani troops that were too far from their bases were defeated by the Bengali rebels who were aided by the regular Indian army. The new state of Bangladesh proclaimed its independence and was immediately recognized by India. The following year, the Shimla agreement officially ended the third Indo-Pakistani conflict.

India's troubles however, were not over. Blood was again shed in rebellions in Arunachal Pradesh and Assam, where the Tibeto-Burmese populations demanded their independence. Delhi had to send troops, unsuccessfully. At the same time, they had to keep an eye on Pakistan which was demanding self-determination for Jammu-Kashmir, as well as on China which was demanding the restitution of northern Arunachal Pradesh. India, meanwhile, refused to recognize the annexation of Askai Chin, which it still hopes to recover.

Matters have become even worse since the seventies, when Pakistan, India and China all became nuclear powers. Border conflicts have not been settled and old resentments remain. Until the fall of the Soviet bloc, Americans and Russians continued to add fuel to the fire for strategic reasons, maintaining "the war of the glaciers," a masked, undeclared war that produced victims on both sides. There were daily encounters and since 1980 the number of incidents has increased. The Indo-Pakistani tension has been at its height since 1990 and is maintained at that level by governmental propaganda from both sides. Afghan mujahiddin have been lending a helping hand to Kashmir rebels, supported by Islamabad, now that their war against the Soviets is over. China affirms that it will not let India impose its rule in the area and is strengthening its ties with the Himalyan states of Nepal and Bhutan. This greatly irritates India which is eager to extend its influence further into the mountains, even at the expense of those two states. Has there not been an increase in the economic and political difficulties of these states and their powerful southern neighbor over the last few years?

The world today, happy as it is to have the cold war ended, does not seem to be paying enough attention to the sound of boots echoing in the Himalayas. One can only hope that man's folly will not one day set off a catastrophe that will destroy the abodes of the gods.

II

The Western Himalayas

from Chitral to Himachal Pradesh

The western Himalayas appear as a more or less parallel massive alignment of mountains oriented northwest southeast. The main ranges are the Karakorum range and the Himalayas themselves, separated by the course of the Indus River. This region contains several hundred summits close to or over 23,000 feet and it enjoys a relatively dry climate, as the position of the Himalayan crescent protects it from the winds and monsoons, or at least diminishes their effects. These climatic features increase as one moves westward, producing predominantly dry temperate, even arid, vegetation. Other mountain ranges continue to the northwest, the Pamirs and the Tianshan in central Asia and the Hindu Kush, which occupy the entire northeast region of Afghanistan. The Hindu Kush are not part of the Himalayas. However, the northern part of their eastern flank which extends into Pakistan is of interest to us, because it forms the junction with the Himalayan chain where the latter, bent and broken by the collision between India and Asia, gave way to the northward thrust. This extremely high region, (the average altitude is close to 18,000 feet), should be considered with the Himalayas, from which it originated.

Sheep and goat raising is one of the main sources of Kalash income.
All the tasks involving animals are done only by men,
reputed to be "purer" than women.

The eastern Hindu Kush is dominated by the hieratic Tirish Mir (25,328 feet), the highest peak of the chain, located in Pakistan. Its snow-capped peaks tower over the deep valleys carpeted with sparse steppe vegetation. The monsoons have little effect here. The countryside is austere. The western slopes have alpine type vegetation, and tend to be more arid, whereas the eastern slopes which get more rainfall, are covered with coniferous and thorn forests. Above, extends the vast high-altitude steppe. This area was part of the Pakistani N.W.F.P. (*North West Frontier Province*). It is called Chitral, after the name of the small Muslim kingdom that managed to maintain its independence until 1947, when it joined the Republic of Pakistan.

Chitral is of particular interest as the home of a surprising, mysterious people, the Kalash, who obstinately refuse to embrace Islam despite increasing pressure from their neighbors.

Who are the Kalash?

The Kalash are a people of shepherds and farmers inhabiting the three valleys of Chitral. The other Pakistanis call them *Kafir* ("pagans"), taking up the old Afghan term used to designate the hillmen of Kafiristan ("Land of the pagans") in the eastern Hindu Kush. At the end of the 19th century, Kafiristan was rebaptized Nuristan ("Land of the Islamic lights"). Thus, there are no longer any *Kafir* in Afghanistan, only Nuristani, all of whom have converted to Islam. On the other hand, the Kalash, to whom they are closely related, continue to perpetuate the ancient traditions. There are, moreover, frequent contacts between these peoples, who communicate over the high mountain passes along the Afghano-Pakistani border.

The origins of the Kalash are not clear. They are Indo-Iranians most likely related to the early Dards, who settled in groups among the foothills of the Hindu Kush in ancient times. These mountains are surprisingly similar in appearance to Greek landscapes, which explains the impression of Alexander's soldiers who, in the 4th century BC, when they saw the European physiognomy of the indigenous tribes, were convinced they had found "the sons of Dionysos". According to the legend, the god, aided by the hero Heracles during his Indian voyages, had left behind some of his compagnons to "colonize" a region that resembled Greece, called Caucasus, and that the Macedonians thought they had found.

They were, in fact, the early ancestors of the *Kafir*. It is believed that in the 10th century certain clans, descendants of Aryan tribes, which had lived in the plains and the highlands of Kabul and Jalalabad for over ten centuries, refused to convert to Islam, which had been brought in from the West. They then emigrated northeastward looking for shelter in the Hindu Kush. Their off-spring, however, were quickly caught

The pagans of the eastern Hindu Kush

up by the religion from which their forefathers had fled. Over the centuries, they tried to defend their traditions as best they could, but in the 19th century, the sultan of Kabul, Abdul Rahman, after massacring a great number of *Kafir*, ordered the survivors to renounce their religion. Many yielded, but those unwilling to accept the law fled in groups through the eastern passes of the Hindu Kush to Chitral, a region not easily reached. The local king (*methar*) allowed them to settle in three distant valleys, Birir, Bumboret and Rumbur, which became their sacred valleys. This is where the one thousand three hundred last *Kafir*, by the name of Kalash, live today.

Their culture

Kalash culture is a survival of the distant past. Their society is governed by a strict moral and religious code which clearly defines all that is pure or impure. This results in a very complex system of obligations and taboos, of purificatory rites and propitiatory sacrifices which each member must follow under penalty of exclusion from the community. The most important person is neither the chief of the clan or village, but the *dehar*, a sort of priest-initiator-guardian of the ancestral tradition. He intervenes through ecstatic transes in the occurence of supernatural events indicating agression from the impure occur, such as epidemics, natural catastrophes, maledictions, etc. The community obeys decisions made by the council of elders, in which the *gadera* ("great men") occupy a choice position. Before these notables can be recognized as such by their fellow tribesmen, they must prove both their great generosity during feasts and ceremonies and their oratorical talent.

Unlike Muslim monotheism, the Kalash embrace many gods. In the beginning Khodai created the earth, then, the other gods and finally, horses who were to serve as their mounts. He then asked the five primordial angels to create man out of clay. After a series of mishaps, man appeared. Khodai called him Adam. He then shaped the first woman, Bibi Awa. Influenced by the serpent, the two humans made love in spite of Khodai's orders, and he punished them by exiling them for five hundred years, one to the east and one to the west. When their penitence was over, he asked the angels to reunite the couple in the center of the world, that is, in Kalash country.

Ever since, the descendants of Adam and Bibi Awa have lived in the sacred land, honoring all the gods Khodai gave them. Those most venerated are, Sajigor, the protector of the herds, Balumain, the conductor of the Kalash people, Mahendeo, the intermediary prophet between man and the gods, Jestak, the goddess of tradition, and Jach the goddess of fertility. A multitude of genies, fairies, as well as a host of mischievous, friendly, and evil spirits inhabit the forests and rivers.

This explains the caution with which the Kalash fell trees, construct bridges or choose a site for building a house –and their constant need to consult the priests. Indeed, they must know the exact limits of the pure and impure in order to woo the divinities of the former and avoid those of the latter.

This division into two mystical realms produces certain surprising results. Thus, women, who normally are socially equal to men, are considered "detestable" when they menstruate or are going to give birth. The blood they lose is a sign of impurity. They are not allowed to live with the rest of the community, considered pure. In every village a *bashali*, or home of Nirmali (the protective goddess of women) has been constructed. Here, in the ritual house for menstruation and childbirth, is where the women concerned must spend the entire period of their impurity.

Their mortuary rites are another remarkable custom. Funerals are one of the most important events in Kalash life, for, if they are conducted perfectly, they allow the soul to join the gods. If they are not, the soul of the deceased runs the risk of wandering eternally between two worlds. The Kalash consider that for a month before his death, the soul of the "future deceased" every night during his sleep, passes over "the invisible bridge of the souls" and visits the Golden Houses of the White Mountain, where he will reside when dead. Once death has claimed him, his body is laid on a bed in the center of the village. As drums beat, everyone comes to bear him a final hommage, while the women of the family lament. The men dance for two days and two nights; for women, there is no dancing. At dawn on the third day a goat is sacrificed. After the final invocations and prayers, the corpse is carried to the cemetery, an impure, magical spot that the Kalash generally avoid. In the past it was customary for the family to erect a wooden statue (*gandaho*) on the tomb. Today, there is only one *gandaho* in the whole Rumbur valley, the final witness to a dying culture.

One of the many Rumber villages. This valley used to have very close relations with the neighboring Nuristani.

They have practically ceased since the Mortimer-Durand line separated the Kalash territory from Afghan Nuristan.

Their future

The future does not look very bright, even if the Kalash refuse to accept the destruction of their society. Their determined resistance is even more praiseworthy as they are surrounded by increasingly insistent Muslims trying to asphyxiate them by every possible means. Modern Pakistan, an Islamic nation, the men, to whom the Islamic faith offers a more important place in society.

Against the obstinate ones who return to the valleys, two redoubtable means of combat have been found: technological progress and schools. Transistors, small agricultural machines and weapons are flooding into the valleys, creating the mirage of mo-

is ashamed of its pagan population and would like to obtain their unconditional surrender, just as the Afghans had done in the last century. To accomplish this, they have increased the red tape for any Kalash who wants to buy land, give a name to his child, get care in a hospital or procure a simple identity card. The authorities have introduced an efficient, offensive system against non-believers. The only road leading into the three valleys is not kept up; as a result, provisioning is difficult and the Kalash have to go down to the Muslim cities. When they do, they are subject to intensive indoctrination by priests who, by cajolery, threats or blackmail, attempt to lure them into the bosom of Islam. Some succumb and never go back to their valleys, even abandoning their families, especially

dern life. At the same time, Pakistani elementary school teachers have been sent to teach the Koran and Urdu to the children, who are more malleable. Unfortunately, the method is proving effective. Since 1960 one-third of the Kalash have deserted their ancestral realm. In the three forgotten valleys of Chitral, there remain only one thousand three hundred diehards: the last non-believers of the eastern Himalayas.

Holidays are always connected to seasonal events and honor the forces of nature. While the men rhythmically strike the drums, the women of Bumboret dance and sing to celebrate the end of the harvest.

The kupas is the big wollen headdress worn by women during ceremonies.
The abundance and variety of the decoration (pearls, bells, mother-of-pearl
buttons, cowries, copper or bronze symbols of the sun) indicate
the wealth and social status of the family.

This woman from the Bumboret valley is preparing the fire for supper
in the kitchen outside her house. She is wearing a shushut, a long headband
enhanced by pearls and cowrie shells that extends down her back.

Some homes still contain mills. Their owners allow them to be used by the people
of the community in exchange for symbolic offerings, for the principle
of giving without exchange is against their custom.

Three generations of a Rumbur family. The grandmother to the right
holding one of her granddaughters in her arms; the mother in the background
and her second daughter to the left.

The last village whose structure remains genuinely Kalash stands at the entrance of the Birir valley.. It is made up of family "cells" which are spread over several floors in a sort of "hive" intended to tighten bonds between members of the community.

The flat-roofed Kalash houses built of stones and dried mud are laid out along the slopes.Hamlets are surrounded by cultivated fields and terraces.

The small outside terrace of the Kalash home is mainly used during
the dry, hot season. This is where the children play, the adults sleep
because it is cool, and the women prepare meals.

The main shrine of the god Mahendeo is situated in the hamlet of Grum,
in the Rumbur valley. It has existed for more than three centuries and the heads
of the horses, mounts of invisible gods, are regularly restored or replaced.

Even the smallest parcel of land won over from the rocks in the valley bottoms
is exploited. Cereals (especially wheat and barley) and fruit (apricots and apples)
are the main crops. Here, the entrance to the village of Brun.

The distant silhouette of Tirish Mir, the highest massif of the Hindu Kush
range which reachs 25,324 feet, dominates the wide Chitral valley. Situated
at an average altitude of 5,900 feet, it has a mild climate which makes it possible
to grow a variety of crops. The inhabitants believe that fairies live in the heights.

Powerful Rakaposhi (25,551 feet) watches over the Hunza valley.
The inhabitants of the region still believe that the massif is inhabited
by fairies who change into vampires when angry.

The Karakorum mountains occupy all of northern Pakistan and in the southeast blend into the Himalayas of Kashmir. They form an enormous barrier, closed off by snow nine months of the year, and were called the "territory suspended between sky and earth", by the ancient Chinese. This massif contains a hundred peaks that reach 19,000 feet, fifteen over 25,000 feet and four "twenty-sixers". Yet, from these seemingly impassable heights, there are paths leading down into the Indus plains that even Neolithic man used. Nature, both majestic and hostile, measures up to the austere mores of the populations living in these high valleys.

The low country and the high country

One can distinguish two main areas within the Karakorum region: to the north the highlands, and to the south the lowlands. The latter are a group of mountains whose average altitude varies between 5,900 and 10,000 feet, flanked in turn, by a series of hills no higher than 5,000 feet. It stretches from the eastern Hindu Kush to the western bank of the Indus. It is marked by high summits, such as Falaksher (20,528 feet), Malika Parbat (17,356 feet), Makra (15,748 feet) and its twin Mussa ka Mussalla. Waterfalls and small lakes are scattered throughout this green wooded region. It harbors some of the most beautiful valleys on earth, particularly the Kaghan and the Svat. There is a relatively mild, pleasant alpine climate. The lowlands are especially nice in spring and the beginning of fall, which is, moreover, the time of important festivities. Winter, on the other hand, is harsh and most roads are closed for four months, whereas the summer is rainy. The monsoons bring water to a fertile soil. The valley slopes are lined with magnificent terraces, all buttressed, dunged and irrigated to grow wheat, sugar cane and a great variety of fruit trees (peaches, plums, grapes, etc.). The upper region, formerly known as the Land of the Fugitives because of its inaccessibility, is the realm of goat and sheep herders. Many are still seminomadic and practice transhumance, leaving for the mountains of the north in early summer and returning to the lower land at the end of fall. Terraces are rarer; the valleys become narrower and end in culs-de-sac against the mountain massif of the highlands that can be reached by elevated passes.

Next there is a radical change in landscape. The average elevation fluctuates between 14,700 and 21,000 feet. Forests rapidly disappear, giving way to granite masses of rugged mountains topped by jagged peaks. These are constantly fragmented by successions of escarpments, ravines, moraines and lakes. The region is riddled with immense hollows of desert expanses covered by meager steppe vegetation. There is a markedly continental climate: very hot in summer

The "suspended territory" of Karakorum

and very cold in winter. Night and day temperature variations can be as great as 35°C. These upper reaches are uninhabited by man. On the other hand, the large valleys that cut deeply into the mountains are well populated, with shopkeepers predominating in the towns, and seminomadic herdsmen beyond.

The region is surrounded by high mountains. Four "twenty-sixers", K2, also known as Godwin Austen or Chogo Ri (28,251 feet), Broad Peak (26,401 feet), Gasherbrum I or Hidden Peak (26,470 feet), and Gasherbrum II (26,361 feet) tower above it. Besides these giants, a procession of other legendary peaks such as Distaghilsar (25,902 feet), Rakaposhi (25,558 feet), Kongur (25,328 feet) or Haramosh (24,547 feet) punctuate the ridgeline. The biggest glaciers in the world, other than those of the polar region, are also found here. Going from west to east, one encounters over forty, one-third of which are over 30 miles long, including the Bathura (36 miles), the Hispar (38 miles), the Biafo (37 miles) the Baltoro (36 miles) and the giant Siachen which dug out a valley 45 miles long!

The vertical wall of the Karakorum forms a natural barrier against the clouds, and thus brings rain to the lowlands it also protects from the glacial winds from central Asia and Siberia. In addition, the course of the mythical Indus flows through deep channels from east to west before swerving abrutly southward towards the Pakistani plains to empty into the Golf of Oman 1,000 miles beyond.

An important section of the Silk Route

Other than Chitral, the principalities of the former Dardistan have always had a reputation for being the richest provinces west of the Indus. Even today, the standard of living of the North Pakistan mountain inhabitants is higher than that of their fellow citizens. These populations are descendants of Caucasoids and Mongoloids. As endogamy is the general rule here, intermarriage has led to surprising ethnic isolates. Living in tribes, these peoples have a warlike, even xenophobic, tradition. Honor, respect for the given word, violent revenge, the supremacy of the paternal clan, and patrilineal transmission of names and land are all strongly anchored in a society based on a strict version of Islam. There is an Ismaili majority, but also a large Sunni community and a restless Shiite minority. The ancient kingdoms had been based on these religious differences and although today the kingdoms have disappeared, the religious rivalries continue, giving rise to frequent conflicts.

Despite the vicissitudes of history, the Karakorum region has, for over a thousand years, maintained its favorable economic position, based on a solid trading tradition. Ancient trans-Himalayan caravan trails, which formerly linked Persia and the Middle East with

China, still crisscross the territory. Many pre-date the arrival of the Aryans. The presence of human sites from the Neolithic along the roads that follow the high valleys of the Karakorum, all natural routes, are proof that prehistoric tribes were already using them. Archeological discoveries have shown that these early men were interested in the movements of the stars and wandered around, without settling down, according to the hunt and the seasons. Later, these first paths were to become trade routes and were used for two thousand years before the Silk Route, of which, moreover, they were to become an important section, even existed. The great caravan trade started with the Achaemenides, was pursued by the Greeks of Bactria, followed by the Scythians, then the Parthians, the Sassanids, the White Huns, the Chinese and the Tibetans. All left in their writings, paintings or sculptures, evidence of their passage, thus making the region a veritable open-air museum with, its special treasures of the Greco-Buddhist epoch of Gandhara (Gumbat, Godgara, Bazira, Butkhara, Loeban, Matelai, Chilas, Huddarga, etc.).

During the ten centuries that the splendor of the Silk Route lasted, the high valleys of the Karakorum were host to passing loads of silk, gold, silver, ivory, precious stones, musk, perfume, spices, arms and countraband merchandise.

The Indus at the foot of the arid Deosai range. This 1,865 - mile-long river originates in Lake Manasarovar in Tibet and flows into the Sea of Oman. Throughout history it has been one of the main communication routes in the Himalayas.

The main axis of this route entered the Himalayas through the Hazara region. From there, it followed the network of valleys whose elevation varies between 5,900 and 7,200 feet. Those most frequented were the Kaghan and the Svat valleys, the latter, renowned for its magnificent landscapes as well as its important Buddhist center. The route followed the Indus, entered the Gilgit valley, the former capital of Bolor, then of Dardistan, which early in history became a central trading crossroad, where goods were stocked either before or after crossing the Himalayas. The trail continued on towards Hunza, another well-known business center, sheltered by powerful Rakaposhi (25,558 feet). This valley was famous for its rubies and pomegranates. Higher up the trail became a mule track ascending the mountains via dangerous, desolate valleys, reaching 19,700 feet, to go over the Khunjerab or Mintaka passes, (which gradually fell into disuse), that led to Kashgar and beyond it to Chinese Turkestan. This section of the Silk Route, that the rigorous climate closed off for more than six months of the year, ceased to be used towards the end of the 15th century, when more practicable maritime routes were discovered. Nevertheless, the older entrepôts continued to be of some importance until the 19th century and have kept their reputations.

The adventure of the Karakorum highway

The *Karakorum highway* is an immense two-lane artery linking Pakistan and China by traversing the Himalayan barrier at the 15,520 foot Khunjerab pass. It follows the old caravan route in all its details. All along its 746 miles, from Havelian in Pakistan to Kashgar in China, it perpetuates the ancient tradition by joining, in the south, the Pakistani *Grand Trunk Road* which then branches out to Afghanistan, Iran and India, and in the north, Chinese Tartary and Tibet.

The construction of the *Karakorum highway* represented man's defiance of nature. Man won, but he paid dearly for his victory. Two lives were lost for every mile of road built. It all began in 1963. For primarily strategic reasons, specifically facilitating troop transportation in case of a conflict with India even during the winter months, Islamabad and Beijing, which had just engaged in conflict with the Indians, each decided to finance half of the construction of a trans-Himalayan route between the two countries. Work began in 1964 on the Pakistani side and in 1966 on the Chinese side. It is difficult to imagine the costly efforts the workers accepted and the difficulties they encountered. Thirty-five thousand men worked for over twenty years in ghastly climatic conditions, endlessly struggling against the giant mountain whose defenses were earthquakes, constant landslides and snowstorms. Hundreds of miles of roadbeds had to be macadamized, twenty-four major

The men will not let anyone else choose and dye the wool used to make rugs and clothes. The work is done in communal tanks which are at the disposal of the villagers.

Sewing is another masculine activity, which may seem surprising for quick-tempered warlike hillmen. Since women are banned from public activities, men must make up for their absence.

Karakorum, like many other areas in this part of the world, is famous for its rugs.
They are always woven on traditional looms by young girls reproducing
the same patterns.Here, in the village of Nominabad.

Despite the efforts of the central government, the Northern Territory remains largely under-developed. Mind-boggling primitive methods are still the only means used to construct or keep up the roads. Even the main roads like the Karakorum highway, were macadamized and asphalted using rudimentary techniques.

During the entire winter many high-altitude roads are closed off by the snow.
In the beginning of the spring, when the snow begins to melt, the first trucks clear
their way through walls of ice and snow, as here, just before the Khunjerab pass.

Pakistani trucks are "works of art". A wood framework is first fixed on
the chassis. Then it is meticulously covered by finely finished metal plates,
patiently chiseled and shaped. Complex lighting, bright colors and garlands
of bulbs add the final touches.

The women, as soon as they are of age to be married, are practically never
allowed to leave their homes. If they have to go out, they can only do so veiled
and accompanied by a member of the family.

Most of the high altitude roads that follow the mountain slopes defy the laws
of nature. Because of the uncertain military situation here, these perilous roads
are constantly used by military convoys. Many accidents ensue.

In the Hindu Kush range the horse is a noble precious animal. But for the
Kalash it represents even more. According to their beliefs,
it is the only mount that the gods consider worthy of themselves.

bridges as well as seventy smaller ones had to be built –the last of which was completed in 1988, although the road was officially opened in 1986.

Today the *Karakorum highway* is fairly busy, although regularly obstructed by huge sections of the mountain that give way, particularly during the July and August rainy season.

The former trade centers on the Silk Route have now become overnight stops, profiting from the manna that renewed trans-Himalayan tranportation provides. This is all the more true as the central government has made a sustained effort to develop the region. Hydro-electric plants, schools and hospitals are being built and the road network is constantly being improved.

On the other hand, many secondary valleys which had formerly been linked to the main trail, gradually became less important. They became increasingly isolated and have reverted to the ancestral values of puritanical Islam. Dir is a typical example: at its apogee, this small city had been one of the main passages for one branch of the Silk Route that went from Bajaur over the Nama pass to Afghanistan, heading towards central Asia and China. Today, Dir is a sleepy, fundamentalist town that one needs an authorization to enter. Like other ancient kingdoms of the region, it is semi-autonomous and has its own sovereign. Generally speaking, because they are quite isolated from each other, the high valleys of North Pakistan have each developed distinctive cultures. Two are of particular interest: Hunza and Baltistan.

The centenarians of Hunza

Hunza and neighboring Nagar, located on the opposite bank of the Hunza river, are inhabited by unusual mountain peoples. For centuries they chose not to mix with other populations, limiting intercourse to exchanges with caravan traders. They gave exclusive obedience to their *mir* (king). When their valley was discovered by Westerners in 1880, it was described as the Shangri La of the Karakorum. The calm beauty of the land, the fertility of the soil which brings forth abundant crops, particularly apricots, which are the basis of local diets and the continuation of pre-Islamic celebrations in this Ismaili community are factors that still enchant foreigners.

There is yet another reason for Hunza's fame. Here, people live much longer than anywhere else. The region is, indeed, famous for its centenarians. It is said that they owe their longevity to the fact that they drink only goat's milk, eat only apricots and they do not smoke or consume any alcohol. Doctors who have studied the inhabitants of the valley have, in fact, noted that the flu, rhumatism and tuberculosis are entirely unknown there. A British researcher, Mac Carisson, carried out a surprising experiment. First, he divided one thousand two hundred rats into three equal groups. He gave the first group only dried apricots, sprouted seeds, a little dried meat, and milk, all of which constitute the basic diet of the people of Hunza. The second group had wheat patties, cooked vegetables, meat with spicy sauces such as the Pakistani eat, and tea with milk, which comprise the normal Pakistani fare. Finally, he gave the last group typically English food. A short while later he observed the following results: the "Hunza rats" were in perfect health, the "Pakistani rats" were prolific and nervous, showing serious deficiencies; and the "Europeans" presented a fairly complete range of common diseases!

The explanation of the Hunza people's happiness may well be in their particularly healthy lifestyle. They seem perfectly at ease in their culture which successfully combines the requirements of Ismaili Islam and belief in the omnipresence of natural genies inherited from their distant past.

Forgotten Baltistan

Baltistan is a tormented arid mountain region, deeply incised by a succession of five narrow valleys (Shigar, Skardu, Rondu, Khapulu and Kharmang) that branch off the Indus. It is located at the foot of the icy, jagged walls of the Karakorum and its entire history can be summarized in a single word: forgotten. Archeological excavations have proven that the Silk Route, which, by following the course of the Indus, should have gone through this region, slighted it, preferring to take the Khunjerab pass. For centuries, nothing was heard of the region until the 9th century, when it became an integral part of Tibet, called Little Tibet. When, during the 16th century, as the Muslims advanced, Ladakh (with which it had been incorporated) abandoned it, even stealing its name and leaving the five valleys

The physical characteristics of the Pakistani mountain dwellers confirm their Indo-Aryan origin, with an evident predominance of the Caucasian phenotype. Despite the later arrival of Chinese and Tibetans, the original type has remained pure.

In all the Hunza village (here in Karimabad) apricots are put out to dry
on the flat roof tops. It is said that this fruit, which is their staple,
may well explain their exceptional longevity.

without an identity. The area only resurfaced in the middle of this century, and as no one knew what to call it, it was named Baltistan, "country of the Baltis", after the dominant ethnic group. The inhabitants are undeniably of Tibetan origin, even if late intermixture with Indo-European and Mongol populations altered the original phenotype. They were converted in the 16th century to Shiite Islam by the Kashmiris; from it they derived their severe, suspicious austerity. However, Muslim rigor is mixed with pre-Islamic beliefs, such as a surprising adoration of fairies. These people are traditionally endogamous, and the high percentage of intermarriage contributes further to their isolation. They lead a hard life, growing wheat and barley on meager plots of land along the Indus and its tributaries. They are extremely suspicious of the outside world and perpetuate an ancient system of customs, such as crossing the Indus on *zacht* (rafts carried by inflated goatskins), as their ancestors did two thousand years ago.

Baltistan is also known as the "closed country". Indeed, until the *Karakorum highway* brought a road to Beshum and opened up the region, one could only get there by climbing the 13,780 feet Shuntar pass or the 13,343 feet Babusar pass! In other words, no one went to Baltistan. Nature, too, presents a single front: arid, desolate, practically without vegetation. The contrast is striking between the ochre and grey mountains where the winds blow dust-filled clouds and the grey-blue waters of the Indus when it is calm, greyish when it scrapes furiously at the vertical cliffs that close in around its tumultuous course.

The spring markets are occasions for the ethnic groups that live in the lower foothills of the Himalayas to come and exchange their products with the mountain people of Karakorum. It is also a time of celebrations and various competitions.

Three Balti children from the village of Bara wearing their typical bonnets.
Balistan, which belonged to Tibet from the 9th to the 16th centuries, before
coming under Muslim control, has kept its traditions, for it remained isolated
from the outside world until the 19th century.

Balistan was formerly part of Ladakh and was known as Tibet-I-Kurd
("little Tibet"). The Tibetan ethnic influence can be observed
in the physical type of the Balti who resemble the Tibetans more than
they do other Indo-Aryan type Pakistani.

Handicrafts are very simple. The same man very often repairs rifles and
makes small pieces of jewelry, soldering metal by makeshift methods. He perfects
his work by engraving traditional patterns.

Balistan is a poor region. Its inhabitants have to work hard to gain their meager
sustenance from the arid, dusty soil. The difficult living conditions have brought
about a very strict, severe moral system and very strong community feeling
among these populations which have been converted to Shiism.

The Shyok in the beginning of November, as it flows towards the Indus.
In the background, the Kaberi and Kondus ranges. As the water level descends
one can begin to see the sand bank in the middle of the river bed,
whereas on the bank the fall harvest is ready.

Many lakes of the region are surrounded by small interlinking canals on
which people move about in shikhara (*pirogue*). Many people with very low
incomes have settled along these waterways.

"Paradise on earth", "Delight of the gods", "Venice of Asia" are some of the titles that have been attributed to Kashmir (today divided between Pakistan and India) by its successive visitors. If one were to add the equally flattering terms of "Switzerland of the Orient" and "Light of India" that have been applied to its neighbor to the east, Himachal Pradesh, one understands that there must be something very special about this Himalayan region which stretches from the eastern bank of the Indus to the Yamuna. Yet, it is literally encircled by the rocky slopes of the Great Himalayas with their desolate, snow-capped peaks. These high mountains, half in Pakistani Azad Kashmir ("Free Kashmir"), half in the Indian states of Jammu-Kashmir and Himachal Pradesh, have an average elevation approaching 19,000 feet to the west and 14,800 feet to the east, with summits such as Nanga Parbat culminating at 26,660 feet, Nunkun at 23,409 feet and Shilla at 23,051 feet. It is a barren, extremely windy zone of no interest to man. Any yet Pakistan and India are fighting for the western part, Kashmir. Twice already, their armies have faced each other on the glaciers, and a third war seems to threaten. It is not, therefore, at the summits that one must seek what has so seduced generation after generation, but in the valleys at their feet.

A land blessed by the gods

It is certainly not a coincidence if all the great Moghul emperors made Shrinagar their summer residence, or if the English chose Shimla. When the former set out, their voyages became veritable expeditions, requiring hundreds of animals and thousands of porters. They built splendid gardens with evocative names, such as Shalimar Bagh ("Garden of Love"), Nishat Bagh ("Garden of Pleasures"), or Nasim Bagh ("Garden of the Morning Breeze"). Whoever has read Rudyard Kipling knows how much the British adored Shimla, where they played polo and which was the summer capital of the Indian Empire.

Even today, this whole area of the Himalayas attracts winter sports lovers to its resorts and, in summer, the crowds of city dwellers fleeing the stuffy humidity of the monsoon-drenched plains, not to mention the many foreign visitors, lured by the secret charm of valleys that lead to the Himalayan summits, as well as by the beauty of the numerous mountain lakes.

This land is said to be blessed by the gods. According to an ancient legend, once a great lake, Satisar, lay where Kashmir lies today, surrounded by a high mountain. The lake was dedicated to Sati, daughter of the Himalayas and wife of Shiva, known as Parvati ("the Mountain One"). Both men and *naga* (half-human, half-serpent chthonic divinities) dwelt peacefully on its banks. But, Jalodbhava, an evil giant rose up from the depths and sowed terror among them. Alert-

The happy valleys of Kashmir and Himachal Pradesh

ed by their lamentations, Vishnu came and split the mountain in order to empty the lake. When its bed was dry, the god slew Jalodbhava. Peace returned to the region and Vishnu and Shiva promised henceforth to watch over it conjointly.

Himachal Pradesh is a worthy rival of Kashmir. Its name means "land of the mountains and snow". In Hindu mythology it is the favorite abode of numerous deities who flee the noise and agitation of the big cities to rest and meditate on its slopes or summits.

A rich farming region

The fame of these regions rests on the stirring beauty of their valleys. Indian Kashmir is no doubt best known to foreigners, but Pakistanis are well acquainted with the Kunhar, Neelum, Leepa and Jhelum valleys, all located in Azad Kashmir, and Indians all dream of Chamba ("the valley of honey"), of Kulu, of Manali or of Kangra. All have the same enchanting appearance of a lush, green countryside. They are rarely over 6,500 feet in altitude, with a temperate alpine climate. The monsoons, whose gales are generally filtered by the high Himalayan crescent which blocks off the east, arrive in moderate form in Himachal Pradesh and to a lesser degree in Kashmir. Between the end of June and the beginning of September, they pour down regular, moderate rains that never cause damage to the crops. There are other more sporadic rains in winter and spring. Glacial runoff completes the natural irrigation provided by an ample network of waterways.

The upper geological layers consist of fertile sediments and alluvial deposits that guarantee two annual harvests, the *kharif* in summer and the *rabi* in winter. Wheat, barley, high-altitude rice, corn, *jowar* (large millet) and potatoes all grow side by side with saffron, tea and a variety of fruit trees (apricots, apples, almonds, chestnuts, etc.). The population, attracted by the fertile soil and the resulting wealth, is dense. Houses are spread across the countryside, for the small farmers, who represent 78% of the population, cultivate all possible land. There is not a single plot of arable land that is unoccupied. Other Pakistanis and Indians call these happy valleys "the granary of the continent". Consequently, their natural abundance has lured intellectuals and artists (Kashmir was a renowned center for religious studies) and encouraged the emergence of a comfortable middle-class involved in trade. An innate sense of business and the taste for bargaining have made the reputation of these northern traders who inundate the whole southern half of the continent. Which traveler in India has not met a Kashmiri or Himachali merchant? And, one may then ask, what business did he do?

The valley slopes are lined with dense forests, within which are found the greatest variety of conifers

The famous houseboats on Lake Dal in Kashmir. From spring to fall these floating
houses attract many Indians and foreign tourists who come to spend pleasant,
sunny vacations here while the monsoons are battering the rest of the continent.

◀ According to tradition, Shrinagar ("city of Shri", another name for Parvati,
the Shiva's consort), was founded on the Jhelum River by the emperor Ashoka.
The city is crisscrossed by many canals which link it to the neighboring lake.
Boats, veritable floating houses, have come to settle all along these canals.

A traveling musician, sitting near his big silver horns and drum,
is waiting for the bus to Vashit, which will take him to the village where a newly
married couple has hired his services. He might even try to make a little extra
money by telling fortunes as his peers often do.

in all the Himalayas and bountiful fauna, formerly the joy of Moghul and British hunters. Above the timberline stretch green meadows, with such poetic names as Sonamarg ("Golden Meadow") and Gulmarg ("the Rose Meadow"), and in the springtime flowers of all colors blanket their slopes. Goat and sheep herders bring their livestock here. Many lead a seminomadic existence, living in tents and following ancestral trails alongside the mountain roads. They reach the summer pastures at the end of May and return to the lowlands in the fall. They know no national borders. The lifestyle of the nomads in the west is seriously threatened by the Indo-Pakistani conflict which is dragging on in Jammu-Kashmir and is cutting off the traditional transhumant trails.

The high valley of Garam Chasma is never lower than 8,200 feet. Shut in by a cirque of mountains accessible only by very high passes, it shelters a population of farmer-herdsmen with very strict moral standards.

III

The central Himalayas

from Kumaon to Nepal and from Ladakh to Tibet

The central Himalayas are often called "the Roof of the World", a phrase which used to refer to the Pamirs until the day when men realized that the highest mountains in the world were the Himalayan chain. The stupendous mass of the central Himalayas, which here reach their maximum width, includes more than eighty peaks over 23,000 feet and eight "twenty-sixers". From west to east they are Dhaulagiri (26,811 feet), Annapurna (26,545 feet), Manaslu (26,781 feet), Gosainthan or Shisha Pangma (26,299 feet), Cho Oyu (26,749 feet), Everest (29,029 feet, called Chomolungma by the Tibetans and Sagarmatha by the Nepalese), Lhotse (27,940 feet), and Makalu (27,766 feet). Awe-struck by the giant mountains, the Hindus and Buddhists made it the abode of the great gods; nowhere on earth could a worthier domain be found.

The central Himalayas receive more seasonal monsoon rains than their western neighbors. Big clouds, held back by the mountain barrier, accumulate on the southern slopes as early as April and May, thus causing evening storms. The abundant monsoon rainfall in July and August accounts for the rich vegetation. Conversely, the high plateau of Tibet and the valleys lying on the northern slopes of the range, and thus protected from the monsoons, receive very little precipitation, except during the short rainy season in July. Vegetation is sparse and in places it even disappears completely to give way to a mountain subdesert, the ultimate stage before the line of perpetual snow at the summits.

After Betravati, going up towards Langtang, one discovers some of the most beautiful panoramas of Nepal. As far as the eye can see there are terraced rice fields. In the background, the lofty peaks of the Great Himalayas.

The territory lying between the Sutlej and the Kumaon range in the west and the Sikkimo-Nepalese border on the east, forms the southern side of the central Himalayas. It appears to be a gigantic piling up of mountains which rise from the hot, tropical forests to reach the frozen heights of the Roof of the World. Such climatic variety is not to be found anywhere else in the Himalayas. Specialists usually divide the entire length of the Himalayas into six or ten climatic stages, but here, that number should be doubled, as each is subdivided into several micro-climates which give birth to remarkable plant life.

T he phrase "stairway to heaven" is commonly used to describe the amazing succession of mountains down whose slopes run numerous rivers. To simplify matters, we shall define four roughly parallel "steps" oriented northwest southeast, each having very distinct features.

The first one represents about 35% of the total area. It begins in the warm, humid lowlands of the Himalayan piedmont, formed by the northwestern part of Uttar Pradesh and Terai. It ends at an altitude of about 3,900 feet in the Siwalik Hills whose bold ridges, however modest they may be, extend over a width of about 18 miles. This region, which receives heavy monsoon downpours and is crisscrossed by a network of rivers, is often flooded. It is covered with lush vegetation whose tropical characteristics diminish with altitude. The Siwalik Hills are distinguished by long narrow valleys parallel to the crestlines, themselves covered with sparse, stunted vegetation. These valleys, called *dun* in Nepal, are said to be unhealthy and despite their fertility are inhabited only by outcastes.

Until the nineteen-fifties, the dense forests had an abundant animal life. That decade, however, marked the beginning of ambitious land development projects. In order to desalinate and cultivate the land, deforestation was widely resorted to. This economic choice has not only pushed back the forest, which has completely disappeared from the zones near the

The stairway to heaven

plains, but it has also dramatically decimated the animal species. Furthermore, it has attracted an uncontrolled mass of people who have made the Himalayan foothills one of the most densely populated regions of the continent, with an inevitable trail of problems (poverty, sky-rocketing birthrate, disease, and insecurity). Rice, sugar cane and fruit trees (banana, mango, papaya and citrus fruits) are grown here.

The second step, between 3,900 feet and 7,200 feet above sea level (the elevation of the first hills of Mahabharat Lekh) represents 25% of the land. It corresponds to the most fertile belt and the most propitious to human settlement. Consequently, two-thirds of the mountain people of the southern slopes of the Himalayas have settled there. The warm temperate climate has produced evergreen forests, although deforestation is now also widespread. For generations, the inhabitants built tens of thousands of terraces up the mountain slopes in order to cultivate cereals, especially rice and barley, as well as orchards (orange, apple, and apricot), thus giving Nepal its unique landscape. The practice of crop rotation relieves the soil and two harvests a year are possible, thanks to a perfect irrigation system and regular seasonal rainfall.

The third step rises up to 16,400 feet, and the line of perpetual snow, in the heart of the Great Himalayas. It represents about 30% of the total area. Several climatic stages succeed one another from subalpine to subnivean. Plants have to adapt to a cold, but also humid, climate characterized by light, frequent snowfalls from fall to spring. The predominantly oak and coniferous forest is less dense and the nearer one gets to the upper belt, the more conifers there are. Above 11,500 feet they gradually become rarer, and eventually disappear at an elevation of 14,800 feet, where the first alpine meadows are to be found.

Human activity is limited by the 9,800 feet mark below which a rather large population of farmer-shepherds live. Their dwindling farming incomes are now counterbalanced by those drawn from goat and sheep raising. On the other hand, in the highlands above this limit, where harsh climatic conditions prevail (for nearly six months of the year snow interrupts all human activity), there are only small, scattered settlements. Agriculture is confined to the inhabited valley bottoms (below 11,500 feet) and produces only one harvest annually. Apart from potatoes which can be grown up to an altitude of 13,800 feet, barley and buckwheat are the only crops. Herding is the basis of this meager subsistence economy. When one reaches the high northern regions inhabited by peoples of Tibetan origin (Thak, Langtang, Solu-Khumbu) goats and sheeps are replaced by yaks and their various hybrids.

The last step begins at the nival level. The area covered by this bleak frozen territory hardly represents 10% of Nepalese land. It lies against the Himalayan wall separated from the Tibetan plateau by a majestic avenue of "twenty-sixers". Despite the extreme elevation of the central Himalayas, their location in the intertropical zone accounts for the fact that the glaciers surrounding the high peaks are fewer and considerably smaller than in the neighboring Karakorum range (the longest one, the Ngojumba, is less than sixteen miles long and the famous Khumbu glacier is only eight miles long). No permanent human settlement is possible in this most inhospitable region. Only the very deep river valleys that run through the entire range and the high-altitude Khung, Larkhya, Thaple and Nangpa passes, which connect Tibet with Nepal or India, are periodically used by rare yak caravans, when climatic conditions are favorable. Trade, once relatively important along these natural routes, has dramatically decreased since the sixties. The objects of this trade have changed little over the course of centuries. Tibet continues to export untreated yak wool and salt to India and Nepal, while importing, in return, cereals and manufactured goods.

In early spring, the beautiful valley of Trisuli, displays its terraces. This region, which is one of the most fertile in Nepal, produces much fruit and two harvests a year of cereals, rice and corn in the fall, and wheat and barley in the winter.

Contrary to a generally accepted opinion, most of Nepal does not get any snow
during the winter. In December and January the fields are covered with white
frost, but the sun soon disperses the morning mist.

In Nepal, terraces (here near Barabise), where rice is the main crop below
4,900 feet, and barley above, are kept up all year long. Each year new terraces
are added, thereby making the Nepalese landscape unique.

Nowhere more than in the central region does the country merit its name
of "stairway to heaven". With differences in elevation of over 4,900 feet,
the terraces of sparkling greens and ochres creep up as though to reach the skies.

There are two varieties of cultivated rice, ordinary and sticky. The paddy,
one of the most common foods, is dried rice which has been separated from
its straw by being stamped on by oxen or buffaloes.

Nepal is not only the land of happy people living in harmony with their gods, as foreigners rushing through too often tend to believe. The kingdom is one of the poorest countries in the world. Its GNP is $170 per capita, with an annual growth of about 4%. The illiteracy rate is as high as 75%. Nepal holds the record for its lack of medical and educational equipment. Its road infrastructure is totally inadequate and investment in scientific research is nil. This underdevelopment has four different causes: very low agricultural incomes, overpopulation, the enormous debt and the geostrategic position of the kingdom. The Nepalese economy is traditionally based on agriculture, which employs nearly 90% of the population and whose products represent 60% of the GNP. However, just over one-fifth of the territory is cultivated, despite a relentless determination to cut down trees which has resulted in serious deforestation below elevations of 8,200 feet. All the rest of the country is covered with sparse forests and meadows or lands that are unexploitable either because of climatic conditions or the aridity of the soil. In addition, mountain societies are traditionally reluctant to change their ways and the government is unable to take drastic measures to diversify the country's economy. In spite of the different land reforms and, since 1987, of a new popular awareness of the problems, the conjunction of all these factors, which continue to worsen, has led the Nepalese economy to the verge of ruin. Nepal's second handicap is its sky-rocketing demography. The 3% annual growth rate has resulted in an enormous increase in population for whom the land cannot provide subsistence. The high infant mortality rate (13,3%) and the low life expectancy (around 52 years)) cannot compensate the disastrous effect of the birth of another 320,000 mouths to feed every year. This is not a new phenomenon. Even before independence, the British spoke of the exceptional fertility of the Nepalese population. Nor are the consequences new.

Overpopulation is not only the cause of general, continued impoverishment, but it also forces many Nepalese to emigrate. For decades, the Himalayas as a whole, and the eastern part in particular, have been the scenes of a vast Nepalese diaspora. Tens of thousands of Gurkhas, Nevars, Tharus, Sherpas and other Rais can be found in Sikkim, Bhutan and Assam where they form an easily exploited "lumpen proletariat" and are an easy prey for local political propaganda. No wonder, Nepalese are involved in the protest and autonomist movements in the eastern Himalayan states. But, as they are foreigners, albeit long-standing residents, they are among the first victims of repression. This is especially true, as the natives, generally Tibetans or Tibeto-Burmese, object to what they consider a deliberate invasion of their lands (for

III
The central Himalayas: from Kumaon to Nepal

One of the lowest incomes in the world

economic and political reasons) and never miss an opportunity to show their hostility to the "immigrants". The antagonism between the different ethnic groups and cultures leads to confrontations which have tended to increase in the last ten years and to destabilize further a sensitive region under careful watch from both China and India.

Another cause of Nepal's economic difficulties is its indebtedness. Its foreign debt attains 1.7 billion dollars, in other words, more than half of its GNP. Despite aid from China, Japan and Western countries, and also considerable trade with Bangladesh and Sri Lanka, the kingdom has not been able to free itself from the political and economic domination of India. Not only is it helpless in controlling the massive influx of Indian workers into the southern lowlands, but, under pressure from India, it has also had to give up its independence with regard to international trade. Moreover, India benefits directly or indirectly from a significant part of Nepal's natural resources (iron, copper, lead, zinc and cobalt) and especially from its hydro-electric power. The dams built on the main Nepalese rivers (the Kali Gandaki, the Rapti, the Sapta Kosi, the Trisuli, etc.), often with Indian financial and technical aid, provide only slightly over 250,000 kilowatts annually, a small proportion of which is exported towards the neighboring countries, mainly India, which enjoys preferential rates. Finally, Nepal's strategic position between the two rival giants and major regional powers, China and India, does not help matters. On the contrary, as India and China are involved in various border conflicts, they tend to keep a closer watch on all the Himalayan states and, above all, Nepal, the largest among them. Nepal has tried to maintain its independence by establishing ties with other countries, such as Rumania, Japan, and Germany, by signing trade agreements with Bangladesh, Bhutan, Sri Lanka, by trying to balance its relations with China and India, by attracting to Kathmandu the secretariat of S.A.A.R.C. (South Asian Association for Regional Cooperation) and the conference of non-aligned nations, and by getting a seat on the UN Security Council. Despite all its efforts, Nepal remains in the sphere of influence of India, which does not hesitate, when necessary, to make its authority felt. The last conflict between the two countries is a good example.

In 1988, the kingdom, stifled by massive importation of low-priced goods from India, decided to impose protectionist tariffs in order to defend its own products. Delhi immediately reacted by imposing a strict economic blockade which brought the country to its knees. The Nepalese government had to abandon most of the measures. India keeps a close watch on everything in anyway related to the armed forces, as it does not tolerate the slightest threat on its northern borders.

◄ Ninety percent of the Nepalese population earns its living from farming and livestock raising. However their income is so modest that their standard of living is one of the lowest in the world.

▲ A Dolpo woman. This ethnic group of Tibeto-Mongol origin inhabits four isolated valleys in the high dry plateau to the north of the Dhaulagiri massif. They grow barley, the only cultivable crop, and raise yaks.

The intensive deforestation of the Lesser Himalayas to gain cultivable land
has brought about a serious shortage of wood. Today, it is sometimes necessary
to go very far from one's village for the daily supply, as these women
from Tashi Palkhel are doing.

The markets of the Kathmandu valley, here in Bhaktapur, abound in fruit
including citrus fruit, which are relatively rare in the mountain regions. They
come mostly from the lowlands and particularly from Terai.

The Nepalese society is based on a system of castes inherited from Hinduism.
Although social compartmentalization is less strict than in India,
those who have the most discredited jobs live together in certain quarters.
Here, the potters' quarter in Kathmandu.

*The heart of the old city of Kathmandu is very colorful and picturesque,
but here one also realizes how meager the resources of these people are and how
ready they are to do any kind of work to make a few rupees.*

Hinduism is omnipresent in Nepalese architecture and sculpture. Their designs
are derived from well-known myths and the organization of forms and volumes
follows religious canons. Here, a detail from the Devi Kumari palace

Hinduism is the religion of the vast majority of the population in northern Uttar Pradesh and in Nepal. This part of the Himalayas harbors some of India's most sacred sanctuaries. From two little towns, Hardvar (one of the seven sacred towns of Hinduism, where a *khumba mela*, the biggest festival in India, takes place every twelve years) and Rishikesh (which counts over sixty *ashrams*), lying at the base of the Himalayan foothills, millions of pilgrims set out every year between May and October, the only time this region is accessible, for the sacred places of Yamunotri (the source of the Yamuna), Gangotri (the source of the Ganges), Kedarnath (dedicated to Shiva) or Badrinath (dedicated to Vishnu). The roads suitable for motor vehicles soon give way to gravel tracks, then to steep footpaths that have to be climbed on foot. These processions winding their way along the hillsides provide amazing scenes of fervor and rites of self-mutilation.

The kingdom of Nepal is the only Hindu country in the world, since in India there is separation of church and state. Hinduism is the state religion of Nepal. It accounts for the structure of society regulated by the caste system and it conditions the life of every individual. The king is considered an incarnation of Vishnu. However, early Hinduism has been deeply influenced by the presence of Buddhists in most major central valleys and particularly in numerous Tibetan communities all along the northern border of Nepal. These communities represent 12% of the population. The influence of Buddhism, the religion of nearly one-third of the Nepalese today, is so strong that one can talk of Nepalese Hinduism or even Himalayan Hinduism, since it has spread beyond the western border of the country. This form of Hinduism, characterized by great tolerance, has a syncretic vision of ideas and forms and accounts for the local people's open friendliness, one of the charms of the central Himalayas.

The abode of the gods

Hinduism places the central axis of the world, the legendary, invisible Mount Meru, which is reputedly directly under the North Star, in the middle of the central Himalayas. Set on the back of the tortoise Akupara, known as Mandara, it served as a pivot for the gods during the primeval churning of the Milky Ocean. According to the legend, it has a height of 84,000 *yojana* (unit of measure corresponding to a day's walk, varying according to place and time, that is between four and ten miles) and it reaches equally far down into the depths of the earth. Mount Kailasa (22,031 feet), called Gangrinpochhe by the Tibetans, where Shiva meditates, not far from the source of the Indus, is its earthly form.

Moreover, the shape of Mount Kailasa is identical to the divine *lingam*, a phallic symbol, and inspired the

Himalayan Hinduism

architecture of the tower dominating the main sanctuary of Hindu temples.

The whole Himalayan range is sacred in the eyes of all its inhabitants. The Hindus often call it Himavant, father of Uma ("Light") whom Shiva, in the shape of Parvati ("The Mountain One") married, and of Ganga, the sacred river that fell from the sky into the god's hair, before gushing forth over the earth. Each mountain and each peak has a name referring to a god and possesses its own legend. All the major sacred rivers which run through the north of the Indian subcontinent have their sources in the heart of the central Himalayas: the Indus, the Ganges and its main tributary the Yamuna (symbolized by a beautiful young woman standing on a tortoise), the Kali, the Karnali, the Kali Gandaki, the Arun, the Tista and the Brahmaputra, the "Son of Brahma", as its name indicates, which originates fewer than sixty-two miles from the source of the Indus.

Vedism, Brahmanism and Hinduism

It is impossible to understand Hinduism, whatever its local form may be, and even Buddhism, without taking into account very ancient Vedism. Vedism is the religion of the ancient Aryans. When these Indo-European warring tribes set foot on the Indian subcontinent, they brought with them a remarkably well-structured politico-religious system. We are well acquainted with it, since its basic tenets are contained in the *Veda* ("Knowledge"), the generic name given to the most ancient Indian texts gathered in four essential books (the *Rig Veda*, the *Yajur Veda*, the *Sama Veda* and the *Atharva Veda*), considered by every Hindu as *shruthi* (original "revelation"). Over the course of centuries, a long series of commentaries on these books and of subsiduary treatises was added, refining the philosophical aspect of a religion which, in the meantime, had become the framework of Aryan society. Indeed, the caste system finds its justification in the sacred *Veda*. In them, Prajapati, a divine entity, who existed before all creation, is said to have offered his celestial body in sacrifice (represented by the cosmic giant Purusha) to enable the universe and living beings to exist. His mouth became *brahmana* (the priest), his arms gave birth to *kshatriya* (the warrior), his thighs to *vaishya* (the craftsman and tradesman) and *shudra* (the servant) emerged from his feet. Besides these four castes, there is the confused mass of the "outcastes", the famous *paria* or untouchables, who include the conquered peoples, the slaves, and the *adivasi* ("former inhabitants", that is, the descendants of the original dark-skinned non-Aryan inhabitants of India). Above this rigidly stratified society, Vedism proposes a vast pantheon of gods dominated by the forces of nature. The major gods are Varuna, the master of sacrifices and guardian of the cosmic order, Indra, the thundering god of war and of atmospheric phenomenoa, Surya, the sun god, Rudra, a deity associated with mountains and storms, Agni, the spirit of fire, Vayu, the wind regulator, and Yama, the lord of death. From the 8th century BC onward Brahmanism refined the original system. The Brahminic caste then assumed an inordinate importance, bending to its rule even the kings generally drawn from the ranks of the *kshatriya*. As the depositories of knowledge, guardians of divine law, and keepers of magic, the priests dominated society. They were aware that original Vedism could not survive the many cultural interferences of the peoples defeated by the Aryans and the endless division of castes (*varna*) into sub-castes (*jati*). New texts, especially the *Brahmana*, the *Upanishad*, the *Shaddarshana* ("Six systems") including the famous *Vedanta*, completed the *Veda*, adapting them to new situations. Extremely complex and esoteric religious and philosophical beliefs were then devised. The universe was conceived of as the place of divine creation that was perpetually renewed during long, successive cycles after which it disappeared until a new creator appeared. At the center of this creation was the *brahman* (the "absolute" or universal soul) from which were derived the *atman* ("self" or individual soul). Former beliefs were specified and integrated as parts of the system; they became the determining concepts, such as *samsara* (the infinite cycle of reincarnations to which every living being is subjected), which then gives rise to the imaginary world of *maya* (illusion created by the world

◄◄ *Sitting in front of the outside wall of the royal palace of Lalitpur (Patan), near a statue of the god Ganesha, a* sadhu *smokes some* ganja (*the Indian version of hashish*) *in his earthenware* shilom.

◄

A young Nepalese ascetic devoted to Shiva. He exhibits the symbols of his god: his hair is pulled back in a bun and he has a large rosary and a gilded trident (trishula).

of appearances), generators of error and ignorance or *moksha* (ultimate liberation from *samsara*), which leads to *nirvana* ("extinction" or non-being), a kind of ataraxic heaven. Three modes of thought with distinctive features developed: *jnana* (transcendental and theoretical "knowledge"), *karma* (practical "law of acts", a sort of assessment of previous lives) and *bhakti* ("self-sur-

*The temple-pagoda of Nyatapola is in the center of Taumadhi Tole in Bhaktapur.
This jewel of Malla architecture was erected in 1708 on the order of King Bhupatindra Malla,
one of the greatest builders of Nepal.*

render" or intense devotion by which the worshipper tended to merge into the divine). The different teachers, however, insisted on the complementarity of the three concepts.

For a Hindu, the message is clear. The *atman* has only one wish: to return to the *brahman* whence it came. But the weight of his *karma* prevents it from doing so and keeps returning him to the endless cycle of reincarnations. There are, however, ways to avoid *samsara*: meditation, yoga, devotion and charity. Brahmins have the key to each of these; hence the importance of the Hindu clergy, the only ones empowered to teach the way to ultimate truth.

During the subsequent centuries, Brahmanism evolved towards Hinduism as it is today. In fact, the word Hinduism only appeared in the 19th century, coined from a British term, *sanatanadharma* ("eternal law") that the Hindus themselves used to name their faith. Hinduism very meticulously codifies all of Brahmanism.

Society and individual actions are ruled by a very strict philosophical and religious system whose com-

mandments and rites are symbolized by a multitude of gods. The Hindus are said to have 33,333 deities! In fact, this multiplicity of appearances corresponds to a fundamentally monotheistic conception of the universe in which creation can take on any appearance according to the time and place.

In simpler terms, each worshipper can adapt his own conception of the deity to his own nature, since by worshipping a god, he is honoring a specific form of the universal god.

The main figure of the pantheon is the *Trimurti* ("Three Forms") and its three supreme gods: Brahma, the creator, Vishnu, the preserver, and Shiva, the destroyer- regenerator. In each god there is a feminine part, the *shakti* ("energy", often incorrectly called goddess), which is the active female principle, and the only one able to activate the inert male principle.

Hinduism reached its formal perfection around the 16th century. From that time on, to meet the expectations of new worshippers, it had to renew itself and to incorporate several other religious, philosophical and moral schools (brahmo samaj, arya samaj, Ramakrishna mission), which gave it the distinguishing features it bears today.

Nepalese distinctiveness

From Indian Hinduism, Nepal has kept most of the religious foundation, adding to it elements from earlier animist cults, such as the belief in omnipresent natural spirits which can be tamed or summoned by magical practices. Animism underlies most major religious festivals, all of which are associated with the rhythm of

the seasons, such as Sithinakha, celebrated at the onset of the rainy season, Astami, which ensures a favorable summer, Ganta Karna when evil influences are conjured away from the rice, and Dasain, the most popular Nepalese festival, celebrating the victory of good over evil in the barley sowing season.

The foundations of Nepalese society were laid at the beginning of the 14th century and were completed at the end of the century by King Jayasthiti Malla. The Indian caste system was adopted and adapted. In Nepal, however, the distinctions between the different castes is hardly as rigid as in India and the concept of untouchability is practically meaningless, because the dividing line between the two lower castes and the *paria* has gradually disappeared. Society accepts and recognizes many intercaste "bridges" through marriages or financial agreements. The only realm in which racial purity remains is that of food, especially, "the gift of water". Members of the pure castes (considered *dvija* or "twice-born") may receive sacred water from one another. They are carefully differentiated from members of the impure castes who may not offer them water. Nevertheless, this code is tending to become obsolete because the Nepalese government

◄◄ *Most of the small temples which surround Pashupatinath, one of the most saintly Hindu places of pilgrimages, are devoted to Shiva. The* lingam *(male sex organ) of the god, painted red and covered with the sign OM, rests on the* yoni *(female sex organ) of his consort.*

◄ *Families come to have the bodies of their dead incinerated on the* ghat *(stairs) of Pashupatinath, founded on the banks of the Bagmati by King Bhupalsingh Malla in the 17th century. Every day the smoke from cremations rises from this particularly holy place.*

Standing against the temple of Hanuman, one of the inside courts,
of the present royal palace whose construction was ordered by King Prithvi
Narayan Shah the Great at the end of the 18th century. The foundations
were built under the Licchavi (5-6th century), and the first buildings,
under the Malla (15th century).

The religious and cultural syncretism between Hinduism and Buddhism can be seen in the ritual and religious objects offered to worshippers at the sanctuary entrances. The mixture of artistic styles and the use of various materials and supports have produced authentic Nepalese art.

In the old quarters of Kathmandu the Buddhist monuments are perfectly depicted
in the Hindu icons. The people (here, backgammon players) are busy with their
activites, and seem to make no difference between the two religions.

Within the holy Buddhist sanctuary of Svayambunath a small temple
is devoted to Ajima (Shitale Mata to the Indians, honored especially
in Bengal and Bihar), "The Pure", a goddess of the Newari pantheon
who is believed to offer protection against smallpox.

first legally abolished the caste system, and in addition forbade the creation of new sub-castes, a practice that still exists in India.

It is above all Buddhism which, as early as the 5th century BC, gave Hinduism its distinctive features. Not only do many Hindu gods have their Buddhist counterparts or exist in Tibetan mythology, but both

rible disease by devoting itself to the cult of Shiva. There is also the festival of Samyak, during which the statues of Buddha are invited to a symbolic feast; this gives Shiva worshippers the opportunity to honor the generosity of their god. Lastly, there is the festival of Chaitra Dasain, in honor of the goddess Durga, "the Inaccessible" (one form of Parvati, Shiva's wife), when

Durbar Square, the principal square in the old quarter of Kathmandu, seen here from Hanuman Dhoka. On the left side of the street stands the beautiful Bhagavati temple, built in the 17th century by King Jagat Malla. The building is famous for its corbelled wooden structure and its carved windows.

religions often share the same rites. The same priest may even officiate for both cults. Many religious festivals are jointly celebrated by the two communities which consciously honor the same deities under different forms and names. For example, Rato Matsyendranath, an invocation to the nourishing rain, enables Hindus to pray to Shiva and Vishnu and Buddhists to thank Avalokiteshvara (or Chenrezi in Tibetan, the *bodhisattva* of compassion). In a similar same vein, Naga Panchami honors protective serpents, such as Takshaka Naga, who was swept away by the waters of the lake when Manjushri, the *bodhisattva* of wisdom, split the Chhobar rock with his sword. Infuriated, the serpent bit every creature it met on its way. The gods punished it with leprosy, but it was cured of the ter-

effigies of the goddess Seto Matsyendranath the White are paraded about.

The complex balance maintained between its different religious and ethnic components gives Nepal its identity. It skillfully blends the daily reality of the farmer and the mystical preoccupation of the clergy, adjusting animist beliefs to the great dogmas of Buddhism.

For Buddhists, the large Bodnath stupa is the most important pilgrimage center in Nepal. Like all the monuments of its type, it is constructed on a mandala design. No one can escape the fascinating look of the "Unchanging Buddha" painted on all four sides of the tower.

Five miles west of Kathmandu stands the Svayambunath hill and,
at its summit, the oldest temple stupa in the region. Atop its white dome
is a gilded tower. It is surrounded by several chaitya (secondary shrines)
and is said to have been founded over twenty centuries ago.

The central chain of the Great Himalayas seen from the Nepalese side
with the peaks of Everest (29,029 feet), called Sagarmatha by the Nepalese
and Chomolungma by the Tibetans, easily recognizable by its pyramid-like
shape. It is east of Makalu (27,766 feet).

The names of the giant central Himalayan peaks have thrilled the hearts of whole generations of adventurers, dreamers and daredevil climbers. This domain, combining beauty, mystery and danger could only attract the lovers of extremes. Many were, and still are, the enthusiasts who set out to tackle this vertical world. But the list of those who lost their lives in the adventure is also long. Conquering the highest peaks on earth has long monopolized the attention of people all over the world who have been fascinated by the exploits and tragedies taking place on the "Roof of the World." Almost all the ascents were accomplished from the Nepalese side since, for many years, the Chinese authorities refused access from their territory.

The defeat of the giant Himalayas

Mountaineering in the Himalayas began a little over a century ago, when English and Russian explorers undertook the first assaults on the forbidden realm, where the gods alone lived. Until then, the only rare, audacious climbers to adventure in the vicinity had been the missionaries exploring the trans-Himalayan trails. The first organized expeditions were British; in the middle of the 19th century they sent geographers, botanists and finally climbers to reconnoiter the first heights of the Himalayas. At the end of the century, rock climbing was the fashion, for American and European climbers had just conquered the Rocky Mountains, the peaks of the Caucasus, of New Zealand, of South Africa and of Kenya, and a huge fad was launched. The only summits still offering a challenge were all located on the Roof of the World, upon which all eyes then converged. Although the first attempts were unsuccessful, were often even mortal failures, the number of expeditions and individual attempts by climbers from many nations continued to multiply. The Europeans, Americans and Chinese were the most persistent in their eagerness to triumph. Still, the Himalayas were to protect their loftiest peaks for many years to come. Not one "twenty-sixer" was conquered before the Second World War and no one even went above the fatal 24,600 feet mark, because of the exceedingly rarefied oxygen.

Once the war was over, the flood of expeditions began again. Now they were better equipped and the climbers were well-prepared athletes. Thanks to the aid of local mountain people (among whom the famous Sherpa, "people of the east") who have too often been forgotten, as have their exploits, and thanks also to the contribution of new climbing techniques and modern equipment, it finally became possible to tackle the "twenty-sixers". All the giants succumbed, one after the other, in a little over the decade known as "the golden age of the Himalayas". Annapurna was conquered first, in 1950 by the Frenchmen Herzog and Lachenal. This victory inaugurated a veritable "race

The Conquest of the Roof of the World

towards the summits", first in the central Himalayas, then in the western and eastern parts of the chain. Germans, Americans, Argentinians, Englishmen, Austrians, Frenchmen, Italians, Japanese and the Swiss followed one another on the Roof of the World. In 1953 the Englishman, Hillary and the Sherpa Tenzing Norgay reached the summit of Mount Everest. The same year, the Austrian Buhl, a member of a Germano-Austrian expedition, vanquished Nanga Parbat. In 1954 two other peaks succumbed, K2 to the Italians Compagnoni and Lacedelli, and Cho Oyu to the Austrian Tichy and the Nepalese Pasang. The following year it was Kanchenjunga's turn, on the Nepalo-Sikkimese border, and Makalu, conquered respectively by the Englishmen Brown and Band, and a French team led by Franco. 1956 was an important year for Himalayan mountaineering: Lhotse succumbed to the assaults of the Swiss Luchsinger and Reiss, Manaslu was scaled by the Japanese Imanishi, Norbu, Kato and Igeta, and Gasherbrum II, by the Austrians Moravec, Larch and Willenpart. In 1957 the Austrian Buhl accomplished a new exploit by conquering Broad Peak. Gasherbrum I was vanquished in 1958 by the Americans Schoening and Kauffman, and two years later Dhaulagiri in turn was overcome by an Austro-Nepalo-Swiss expedition directed by Eiselin. The last of the "twenty-sixers" to admit defeat was Gosainthan or Shisha Pangma, which had heretofore been protected by its location in China. After a number of failures and heavy losses, a team led by Xiu Jing triumphed over it in 1964.

A threatened ecosystem

Today the era of the discoverers is over. On the peaks, they have been replaced by top-level athletes and, lower down, by trekking enthusiasts. The result is incredible congestion in the Himalayas. In this respect, the history of Everest is revealing. It is highly venerated by the indigenous peoples. The Hindus call it Sagarmatha ("the one whose head touches the sky"), while for the Buddhists it is Chomolungma or Chomolangma. The former term, used by most of the people and better known in the West, means "Goddess mother of the winds", and the latter, which signifies "Standing goddess" is used by the Tibetan monks forced by the Chinese to leave the Rongbu monastery, located at the foot of the mountain. The monks thought of it as the seat of Thonthing Gyalmo (the "Queen of the Blue Mountain"), one of the five *dakini* personifying Buddha's feminine qualities. When it was first sighted through field glasses in the early 19th century by the British residents in India, it was called Peak XV. Then in 1852 it became Everest, after George Everest, head of a British cartographic mission which had just established that Peak XV was indeed the highest peak on earth. Between 1893, the date of the

125

first attempted ascent, and 1953, when it was conquered, Everest was host to thirteen expeditions. Today it has been trodden on two hundred and eighty-three times by two hundred and fifty-three different climbers, among whom are included forty-two Nepalese (who enjoyed sixty-three victories), twenty-eight Japanese (thirty-three victories) and twenty-eight

peaks. In 1992, the tourist services of Pakistan, Nepal, India and Tibet provided the following figures: two thousand and six hundred, six thousand and five hundred, thirty-two thousand and finally eight hundred *trekkers* respectively travelled the Roof of the World. These countries draw substantial revenues from what is beginning to be called the "industry of the peaks".

One gains access to the pasture lands near Lake Yangdrog Yamtso via the Karo Lo pass, located at an altitude of 16,552 feet among the high massifs.

Americans (twenty-nine victories). They are followed, in order by sixteen Chinese, thirteen Indians, thirteen Germans, eleven Russians, ten South Koreans, nine Frenchmen, nine Spaniards, eight Englishmen, seven Austrians, seven Poles, seven Yugoslavs, six Italians, six Australians, six Norwegians, five Bulgarians, four Canadians, three Czechoslovakians, three New Zealanders, two Mexicans and one Dutchman.

As one can imagine, the route up Everest is becoming congested. In addition, over the past decade a highly new form of mountaineering widely covered by the media has had a spectacular development. It emphasizes the sports exploit that pushes back the limits of what is humanly possible. Thus, we see solitary ascents with minimal equipment and without respiratory devices, as well as sprints and peaks climbed one after the other.

Trekking is also a recent phenomenon and has brought increasing numbers of hikers to the Roof of the World. Although they do not tackle the summits, they can be seen in great numbers along the trails, between 11,500 and 18,000 feet, that lead to the

Trekking directly or indirectly brings to Nepal alone nearly fourteen million dollars. The consequences of this "Himalayan Rush" are well known. The average cost of living has increased in an anarchic manner, in the tourist areas, seriously lowering the purchasing power of the already poor native population. The traditional social system has been destabilized, for villagers prefer to abandon their poorly paid jobs requiring great physical exertion in order to serve as guides and porters for foreigners willing to pay dearly for their services.

And last of all, some trails have scores of insensitive hikers who pollute nature by leaving behind all sorts of garbage. The most infamous of these trails is the *Annapurna Highway*, as it is derisively called by the Nepalese. Around twenty thousand hikers take it annually to do the tour of the massif of Annapurna, whose name means "The one who provides food"! Local governments, however, have recently awakened to the mortal danger that is threatening the Himalayan ecosystem. They have, therefore, taken drastic courageous measures to limit the effects. In Nepal, for ins-

*Kanchenjunga (28,209 feet), seen in the early morning light of December.
This peak, whose name means "The Five Treasures of the High Snow" is the third
highest Himalayan summit. It is on the Nepalo-Sikkimese border in the middle
of the imposing Sangalila range that separates the two countries.*

tance, burning wood in the sanctuaries of Everest, Langtang or Annapurna is now forbidden. Most parts of certain regions have been closed to foreigners, such as Dolpo or Mustang. The same is true for India, which has become very strict about those entering Spiti or Kinnaur and has completely forbidden the whole area of Nanda Devi. Even Pakistan, which is eager for foreign tourist currency, has imposed strict rules for climbing K2 and both Gasherbrums, or adventuring onto Tirish Mir. On the Chinese side most of the Himalayan peaks are still inaccessible.

The Nyanchen Tanghla range, reaching an elevation of 23,255 feet, separates the flat Namtso region from the Damshung gap, which is one of the main transhumance routes used in spring and fall by herds of yaks.

The Himalayan region bordering the Tibetan plateau to the southwest includes
Rupshu, Ladakh, Zanska and Spiti. This area, with its vast succession
of fragmented mountain massifs, resembles a moonscape.

One must not confuse the Tibetan Himalayan area with Tibet itself, of which the moutains are but the southernmost part. They cover roughly 286,000 square miles, or a little less than one-third of the Tibetan plateau, at an average altitude of 13,000 feet. The Tibetan area, so-called because nearly all the peoples who live there are of Tibetan origin, occupies the whole northern part of the central Himalayas. But it also encroaches on the northeastern part of the Western Himalayas and continues all along the northern border of the eastern Himalayas. It stretches along more than 1,200 miles from Ladakh to Tibet and its contours are laid out around the huge hydrographical complex made up of the upper stretches of the Indus and the Brahmaputra.

The southern high plateau of Tibet can be seen as a huge succession of arid lands, whose monotony is periodically broken by folded sedimentary ranges, laid out northwest southeast, parallel to the Trans-Himalayas whose massive shapes reach no further than 19,600 feet. The only possible human activity is herding. Numerous groups of nomads called *changpa* ("the pasture folk") cover these stretches of steppe, stone and sand, in quest of the meager pastures (*chang*) which ensure the subsistence of their huge yak and sheep herds. The yak, the ideal pack animal, and the *drong*, a powerful uncastrated male yak, also give them meat, milk from which a highly-valued type of butter is made and a sturdy wool used to make clothes, "black tents" and ropes. Their hoofs are used for making glue, their dung is a precious fuel and their skins, after being stretched on a wooden frame, are used on the coracles, the frail boats used for crossing rivers and streams. When one nears the Himalayan heights, the *chang* progressively give way to the *brog*, the more numerous mountain pastures where the *brogpa* (nomads living in tents as do the *changpa* and making do with the product of their herds) and the *somabrog* (seminomads who practice transhumance, moving their animals to summer pastures and bringing them back to winter in the valleys) meet. The

A *land of poor mountain folk*

numerous yak hybrids find favor with the seminomads, even more so than the yak, most useful to those who are completely nomadic. The *zo*, born of a yak and a cow, and its female, the *zomo*, which are perfectly suited for work in the fields, and the *dimzo*, a cross between a bull and a female yak, are very useful to them.

In the valleys, one can find the only lands that can be used for agriculture. Bounded by the above-mentioned ranges, they almost all extend parallel to the Himalayan axis. There again, the southernmost lands, close to the Roof of the World, have a more favorable climate. These valleys are inhabited by sedentary, agricultural peoples, called *rongpa*, and three-quarters of them are concentrated in the single valley of the Yarlong Tsangpo. However, the severe climate (the variations in temperature from summer to winter are greater than 60°C), the barrenness of lands whose average altitude is almost 13,000 feet and never descends below 8,200 feet, and the bitter lack of modern technology, allow for only a scanty subsistence type agriculture, possible only during the warm season, from April-May (sowing time) to September (harvest time). The crops which man has managed to adapt to these conditions are limited. One finds mainly onions, peas, *yuanken*, a type of turnip, buckwheat and mostly *tsingke*, a hardy variety of barley, which once roasted and ground, yields flour called *tsampa* which is blended with tea and constitutes a staple in the diet. Some types of cereals (wheat, millet) and potatoes, as well as various fruit trees (jujube, apple and pear) can be found in the lower regions. The products of hunting and fishing occasionally complete the daily diet, but the standard of living remains very low.

The Tibetan region is inhabited by various ethnic groups which can all be called Tibetans, even though some are of Tibeto-Mongoloid origin, others are Tibeto-Burmese and even a few Turko-Mongols.

These populations include multiple clans and groups which do not correspond to one coherent ethnic group, but only to their geographical distribution. In this respect, they are, from west to east, the Ladakhpas, or Ladakhi (including the inhabitants of Zanskar and Rupshu) the Topas (to whom the people of Aksai Chin are sometimes assimilated), the Upas, the Sakyapas, the Trowowas, the Lhopas (not to be confused with the Lopas, "savages", who are groups non-converted to Buddhism and living in the eastern

Nomads coming from the Tibetan plateau who want to reach the Tsangpo gap
have to cross the Nyanchen Tanghla range. There are few passes and they
must travel long distances around the mountains before reaching them.
Their route is lined with campsites (here, south of Damshung).

A large herd of yaks in the Namtso region. Their owners are somabrog.
*They practice thranshumance, climbing up to the pastures in summer
and returning to their valleys at the end of fall.*

Himalayas) and the Monpas ("mountain folk", a term used scornfully). Under this last appellation which, strictly speaking, designates the people of Tawang, are gathered a whole series of Tibetan peoples who live on "the other side of the Tsangpo", that is, in the Himalayan regions which, in the course of history, have been successively attached to and separated from Tibet. The inhabitants of Spiti and Kinnaur in India, of Mustang, Dolpo and Langtang in Nepal, those from the northernmost part of Sikkim and Bhutan, among others, are part of this group.

◀ The Drigungtil valley is typical of the poor isolated valleys which cut across the high Tibetan lands. Rare summer rains have just fallen and the river bottom is thick with grass. The villagers will now have feed for their small herds.

▲ On a cold autumn morning, a Changpa cowherd is drinking his hot tea with salted butter. He has added some tsampa. This drink will be his only one of the day. Meat is reserved for pecial occasions.

Milking the yaks and the zo (a cross between a yak and another bovine)
follows the same ancestral ritual. The men first speak gently to their animals,
then give them a handful of tsampa (roasted barley), before having them urinate
by blowing on their tails. Finally they milk them, thereby obtaining
the precious liquid, the staple of these nomads' diet.

As the first summer rains begin to fall, a caravan of nomadic herdsmen
in the Tinggri valley is preparing to set off for summer pastures. These first rains
are the signal that the meadows must now be green.

In the summer, when the temperatures are mild, the windows at the top of the tents can be opened. Once the "hat", a square piece of material, has been removed, the opening lights the interior and the smoke from the fire can escape.

Life in the villages moves along at a slow pace. Activities have remained the same for centuries. Like her ancestors, this old woman from Gyangtse cards, spins and dyes wool with the help of her granddaughter.

A family of Changpa nomads is gathered inside their yak-hide
tent to share the evening meal of soup and milk products. They are wearing
their winter clothes, chuba, made of animal skins.

These nomads from Changthang have set up their camp north of Yupa.
While the women gather the cow pat which will be used as fuel,
the men attach the animals in a circle around the fire.

In the valleys yaks are used for their milk, their meat and their hides, but
they are almost never used for work in the fields. During the day the animals
are allowed to roam and at night they come back to the village by themselves.

The Spiti River as it traverses Kaza. Although the Spiti region is administered by Himachal Pradesh and constitutes its northernmost section, it is really part of Tibet, whose harsh climatic conditions it shares.

Tibetan nomads have very few precious belongings. They are, however,
particularly attached to certain highly symbolic objects, like this knife
in its engraved sheath, that evokes their warrior tradition.

Ceremonial headdress of Zansakri women. Called perak, these headresses
comprise the family treasure. Turquoises, coral beads and coins are set
in a black felt base which is sometimes reinforced with leather.

Harsh climatic conditions (sun, wind, dust and cold) contribute
to the premature aging of the people's skin. This Ladakhi woman is not
so old as her wizened face would seem to indicate: she is not yet fifty !

As bridges are rather rare, crossing the major rivers is not an easy matter.
Some riverside residents have chosen to become professional ferrymen.
Here they are helping the villagers from Saga cross the Yarlong Tsangpo.

The different valleys of the Tibetan steps are separated by huge mountains, ▶
thus making any communication difficult. In order to go over
these rock walls, the inhabitants must struggle along unstable ground
where small caravans follow ancient mule trails.

Lake Namtso is located at an altitude of 15,062 feet. ▶▶
It is 750 square miles and is the largest salt lake in Tibet
(only Quinghai Hu, in China, is bigger). On its banks, there is
an important Buddhist cultural center that attracts the nomadic peoples.

The Lamayuru monastery was built at the end of the 11th century by Jigten
Gonpo on the site of a former sanctuary devoted to Bonpo. Today a big
community of Drigungpa monks lives there. It is at the intersection
of the Ladakh and Zanskar roads.

All these groups, whether they be Tibetans from the interior or Tibetans from the exterior have developed, in accordance with their natural environment, original forms of their common culture. The Tibetans from the interior created highly diversified houses and the others have developed very distinctive monumental architecture.

Religious architecture, even though it must compromise with its environment, follows first and foremost religious imperatives. Buddhism, originating as it did in India, brought with it Indian architectural elements. Thus, the first sanctuaries were all oriented towards the four cardinal points with a main east-west axis as in the *mandala*, the geometric representation of the cosmic universe. The roof was of carefully laid-out varnished tiles. Later, when Tibet fell under Chinese and Mongolian rule, Asian architectural influences greatly modified the aspect of religious buildings. The well-known, richly-decorated Chinese roof with upturned corners became the norm.

Shortly thereafter, the Nepalese technique of roofs covered with sheets of gilded copper was used in most of the major monasteries and temples, turning the tiles into mere decorative elements placed on the upper terrace-roof. Various religious symbols and gilded animal designs rounded out the whole. Finally, the old west-east disposition changed to north-south so as to make the most of the sunlight. Classical Tibetan religious architecture had come into existence. It was eventually to reach its peak in the construction of some of the most prestigious monumental complexes in the world, such as the Potala in Lhasa (the palace of the Dalai Lamas) and the Tashilhunpo in Shigatse (palace of the Panchen Lamas) in Tibet, the monasteries of Pemayangtse and Rumtek in Sikkim, and the *zong* (monastery-fortresses) in Thimphu and Paro in Bhutan.

In time, the monasteries expanded as the monastic community grew. Subsidiary buildings were added to the main sanctuary, (temples, chapels, assembly halls capable of holding several thousand monks, prayer rooms, libraries, kitchens, monastic cells), enabling their architects to play freely with vertical and horizon-

Religious and domestic architecture

tal recesses and with the facades set back along oblique lines and other orientations. This artistic freedom in the use of lines has given the large buildings their characteristic aspect of monumental flexibility which seems to adapt the imposing mass of the buildings to the lie of the land. Moreover, it allows surprising plays of light consciously sought after by the designers who skilfully combined the use of three principal materials for the facades: painted wood (solid beams or "bundles" of branches), red brick, white roughcast, in order to create a surprise effect and to break the monotony that might be produced.

The Tibetan spirit has found its best expression in the field of domestic architecture. The construction of private homes takes into consideration the climatic conditions which vary greatly from one region to the next, whence its surprising variety. The constant struggle against the cold determined the general "watertight box" shape of the houses. But there is also another important element, essential to any building, the wood, which constitutes the wall and roof frames. However, one of the characteristics of the Tibetan region is a bitter lack of timber. Therefore, domestic architecture is conditioned by the near-absence, or the relative abundance, of wood. To simplify, it can be said that there are two great climatic zones in this region: the upper, dry, alpine zone and the lower, cold, damp, temperate zone. The first yields an essentially rock world where wood is scarce. This zone comprises all of southern Tibet and its western steps: Ladakh, Zanskar, Rupshu as well as northwestern Nepal (Dolpo and Mustang). All these areas are cut off from the monsoons by a high central range, thus turning them into a mountain sub-desert. The temperate zone, which is strongly subjected to the monsoons, has forests rich in timber and bamboo. It includes Kinnaur, Manang, Rolvaling, northern Langtang and Solu Khumbu, and the Kirong, Chumbi, Lhoka, Kongpo, Dagpo regions in eastern Tibet, as well as the northern borders of Sikkim and Bhutan. By force of circumstances, the houses in the upper regions are usually made of stone, those in the lower regions more frequently of wood. All, however, are built according to a

▲
At the foot of sacred Mount Haiburi stands the Samye monastery, founded, according to tradition, in 779 by King Trisong Detsen. It was badly damaged during the Chinese Cultural Revolution and has been beautifully restored according to original plans.

◄ The Yumbu Lakhang castle is said to be the oldest in Tibet. Home to the Yarlong kings since the 6th century, it became a monastery after the fall of the royalty. The legend says it was founded by Nyatri Tsenpo, who descended from the heavens in 130 B C.

The Thiksey monastery is ► one of Ladakh's richest. Built in the 15th century on the ruins of an ancient 11th century sanctuary, it contains seven temples and is home to over one hundred monks belonging to the reformed Gelugpa order.

basic plan, consisting of an either square or rectangular walk-in area, bounded by four load-bearing walls set at right angles to one another. The main door usually faces east. The flat roof is made of beaten earth. This basic module can be extended at will, vertically or horizontally, following the lie of the land and the size of the family. Thus the houses are one or two storeys

the cold. The earthen roof is placed on a course of branches, resting on beams buried in the walls, and whose extremities sometimes protrude on the outside. Occasionally, a central opening in the terrace-roof lets in the sun for light and warmth. In bigger houses, or in ones with a second storey, the various rooms are laid out around this central opening which

The now abandoned palace-fortress of Leh, overlooks the capital of Ladakh. It was built in 1600 by the "lion king" Singge Namgyal. Until the middle of the 19th century it served as residence for the local sovereigns.

high and the second storey sometimes boasts a small balcony. The walls are tapered from bottom to top, giving the larger homes their characteristic "pyramid" aspect. The unevenness of the ground brings about facade recesses and different levels within a home, but this in no way hampers an architecture unconcerned with problems of symmetry or volumetric proportions, but which plays admirably with this unevenness of the ground. The interior lay-out always begins with the kitchen, the most important room. When the first-floor walls (and those of the second floor, where there is one) are finished, the central pillar of the kitchen is erected. The larger houses may have several secondary pillars whose function is essentially decorative. The upper-level floors, made of strips of wood covered with "yak grass" and earth, rest on joists embedded in the walls. Windows are a recent addition, especially in the homes of the common people. So it is with glass, a privilege of noble families. Numerous houses still have no window panes and, in winter, the openings are stuffed with rags.

In the meadows and high mountain pastures, the original type of architecture appears in its most elementary form. The adobe or stone walls are very thick. Windows are few and small, in order to keep out

then becomes an actual inner courtyard, protected from cold winds, where the women can work and be sheltered. The animals live very close to the people to whom they bring their warmth. In the most rudimentary houses, they are penned in folds built along the walls. In the storeyed houses, they are gathered below the second floor, where the family lives.

In the temperate and humid zone, the building materials are timber and bamboo, both widely used in erecting the light, thin, load-bearing walls, full of openings. An adobe coating fills the gaps and waterproofs the whole. The inhabitants often decorate the inside of their homes with brightly-colored religious or mythological paintings, or with fertility symbols, such as the phallic and sexual symbols found in Bhutan. The beams supporting the different storeys, as well as the roof, protrude far outwards and are abundantly sculpted and painted. The first floor comprises the barn and the stable; the second storey and, if there is one, the third storey, are set aside for human habitation; a final space, often with lattice-work, serves as an attic. The flat roof is replaced by a sloping or a double-sloped roof, made of a sturdy frame covered with shingles or slates.

At the intersection of the principal roads leading to Nepal,
India and Lhasa, the town of Gyangtse (altitude, 9,515 feet) was one
of the main Tibetan caravan centers. The city has an imposing
monastic complex dating from the 14th century.

The Gelugpa monastery in Dhankar, built on a high rocky promontory overlooks the Spiti valley. It was greatly damaged during the Chinese Cultural Revolution. Despite the efforts of the villagers and the monks it has remained semi-abandoned.

The main interior court of Tashilhunpo, an imposing monastery,
which was for a long time the residence of the Panchen Lama.
This religious structure, founded in the 14th century by a disciple
of Tsongkhapa, is now home to 700 monks and 200 novices

The Drigungtil monastery is a 12th century kagyupa monastery which clings
to a hillside overhanging the valley. The monks continue the ancient custom
of cutting up corpses and feeding them to the vultures.

The dusty riverbanks of the Yarlong Tsangpo are lined with small hamlets where a poverty-stricken population lives. The main road follows the river. The meager income of the inhabitants comes essentially from animal raising or barter with people passing through.

*Below altitudes of 10,000 feet, wood is widely employed in the construction
of eastern Tibetan houses. Above the top floor there are open gables
used as lofts for stocking fodder and fire wood.*

The insides of the homes are poor, for the people of the Tibetan area earn very low incomes. Nevertheless, the little money they have is invested in copper and pewter kitchen utensils, which comprise the main family inheritance and are proudly exhibited in the principal room of the home.

A typical house of the upper regions of Tibet. It is a one-storey construction
built on a rocky ridge overlooking the Drigungchu valley from an altitude of
15,000 feet. As wood is rare, stone and clay are the main building materials.

Kinnauri homes, whose construction requires much timber,
suffer during the heavy monsoons. Not only the facades, but also
the frames and the internal structures are damaged by the summer
humidity and must periodically be restored.

A Ladakhi village in the Matho valley at approximately 13,000 feet.
The inhabitants have constructed their homes on both banks of a river that rises
in the Matho Kangri range whose glaciers supply water to the whole region.

During the tsetup (*anniversary holiday*) at the Tashichos zong (*monastery*)
in Phyang, *the big* thangka *is traditionally exposed on the wall*
of the main sanctuary for the faithful to see. For the last few years,
however, the monks have not displayed it.

Lamaism is the name given by Westerners to the distinctive form of Tibetan Buddhism (a synthesis of Mahayana and Tantric thought), from the word *lama* which designates a monk of superior wisdom. The Tibetans refuse the term Lamaism and prefer that of *chos* ("law") to define their faith, which they consider an integral part of Buddhism.

The Lesser Vehicle, the Greater Vehicle and the Diamond Vehicle

The name of Buddha ("the awakened one" or "the enlightened") is central to Buddhism and covers two different meanings. The first designates the historical Buddha, Gautama Shakyamuni. The second designates the "Buddha Principle", that is, all of its possible manifestations. *Hinayana*, or "Lesser Vehicle", recognizes only the historical Buddha, whereas *Mahayana*, or "Greater Vehicle", as well as the schools derived from it, believe in the existence of numerous other Buddhas.

The message of the historical Buddha is much more philosophical than religious. It advocates a middle path avoiding both the excesses of asceticism which, by denying the body, mutilates the spirit, and the pursuit of pleasure and of power which "consumes" the human spirit. It emphasizes the common nature of essence and existence, in other words, of spirit and substance, a fundamental concept denied by most major religions which oppose the soul to the body, depreciating the latter.

Another original feature of Buddhism is the necessarily transitory and impermanent nature of every living creature, and consequently of man, in a universal and cyclical dynamic, in perpetual transformation without beginning or end. Human life is a part of *samsara*, the infinite cycle of successive births, deaths and rebirths. The tragedy of man, who does not understand universal impermanence, is to attempt to possess and to keep material goods and power. His inability to satisfy his desires leads to inescapable suffering. He is the victim of the "three poisons": anger, greed and ignorance.

The law of the Buddha (*Dharma* in Sanskrit, *Chos* in Tibetan) offers a way to free oneself from *samsara* and to reach *nirvana*, after having been "awakened".

The adepts of the Buddha's original word gathered together to form the *Theravada* school or "Doctrine of the Elders", which combined the teachings of the historical Buddha within the Pali canon. Although later quarrels caused internal splits, the *theravada* doctrine spread into Sri Lanka, then into southeast Asia (in Burma, Thailand, and Laos, it has remained the major religion; in Cambodia, it was supplanted by the Greater Vehicle). But the main handicap of the *theravada* doctrine was that it was directed at a social and intellectual elite. Indeed, only the scholars, or nobles, had

Lamaism

access to the monasteries where they pronounced the *tripitaka* or "the threefold refuge" seeking asylum in the *sangha* (the Buddhist community), the Buddha and the *Dharma* (the Buddhist law). Therefore, *nirvana* was strictly for the monks. Moreover, monkhood implied celibacy, chastity, renunciation of the world and its vanities, thus excluding laymen. The clergy had understood this and had tried to associate laymen to the *sangha*, but the divorce between the priests and the laymen was too great.

Mahayana or "Greater Vehicle" brought an original solution as early as the 1st century BC. It opened the way to salvation to all men, whether lay or religious, a doctrine contrary to the *theravada* belief, thereafter derisively called *Hinayana* or "Lesser Vehicle" by its rival.

Originally, *Hinayana* and *Mahayana* did not differ much in their doctrines. Both took up the original teachings of the historical Buddha but, while the Lesser Vehicle strove for the salvation of the individual, the Greater Vehicle emphasized the necessary communal solidarity needed to attain the enlightenment of all. For that reason, the new doctrine needed indisputable guides, both enlightened and wise, and yet able to feel human emotions. These "saviors" were the *Bodhisattva* or "Awakened Beings", whose main characteristic was compassion and who were very popular deities in their own right. The original philosophy then became an authentic religion with an ever-increasing pantheon. The Greater Vehicle spread into northern India and Kashmir. From that time on, the schism between the Lesser Vehicle of the southern schools and the Greater Vehicle of the northern schools became irreversible. In its turn, *Mahayana*, in strong competition with Tantrism, subdivided into several rival sects which spread into China, Tibet, Japan, Indonesia, Cambodia (where it replaced *Hinayana*), and Vietnam, where they became original schools.

Originating in the 5th century in northern India, *Vajrayana*, or Diamond Vehicle, is the Tantric form of *Mahayana*, progressively altered under the influence of Tantric doctrines firmly established in Bengal.

Vajrayana sprang from the need to reach a wider public. To do so, it had to absorb magical practices of pre-Buddhist cults and emphasize the preeminence of rites. It combined the physical, psychic and sexual methods of Tantric yoga and the original philosophy of Shakyamuni. It originated in *Madhyamika* or "middle path" a Mahavanist doctrine which denies every certitude about the immovable reality of things and demonstrates the necessarily illusory, impermanent and impersonal character of phenomena. Voidness alone (*shunyata*), not to be confused with nothingness, exists. It symbolizes the non-existence and the non-substance in which all possibles are contained. Above all,

169

Details of some prayer flags hanging from the roof of the main fortified lamasery temple, Dhankar, in Spiti. These flags flutter in the wind and, thus, the sacred mantra are endlessly repeated.

it proclaims the non-differentiation of voidness and form, asserting that no shape or idea can translate the unique nature of the world.

The faithful must then merge into this voidness by breaking down the constitutive elements of all phenomena and by gradually and methodically following the path to Enlightenment. Hence the special importance

Bonpo and Lamaism

When *Vajrayana* reached Tibet in the 7th century, it found a philosophical and religious system already in place: B*onpo*, the former religion of the common people.

In Tibetan, *bon* means "to recite" or "to invoke". This term is used to designate all the religious schools

The Tibetan roads are lined with monuments of various sizes indicating the sacred or magic places. They are called chorten. *Sometimes, simple cairns are enough. These are in the Largeh pass leading to the Namtso plateau, at an elevation of over 16,837 feet. A traveler has stopped in front of the* chorten *to greet it with a handful of snow.*

accorded by the adepts of *Madhyamika* to the rites derived from Indian Tantrism.

This doctrine proclaims the unique character of the world, from the microcosm to the macrocosm, and recommends physical exercises (*laya yoga*) and spiritual exercises enabling the awakening of *kundalini* ("snake" symbolizing the source of all energy) into a sort of sublimation of sexual energies, as well as the systematic repetition of *mantras* (sacred formulas concentrating in material form the spiritual or divine principle they evoke).

Moreover, the name *Mantrayana*, "Path of the Sacred Formulas", is often given to *Vajrayana*. The adept strives to partake in the universal fusion which, by changing itself into a creative force, enables the world to endlessly renew itself.

with a fundamentally animist basis, that existed before the introduction of Buddhism to Tibet. The *bonpo*, then, were "people who recited" magic formulas or epics. Regarded as kinds of bards by Buddhists, the members of the *bonpo* clergy were originally shaman-priests whose main functions were divination and funeral ceremonies, two privileged moments of the magical contact between the real world and the invisible. Their numerous powers and their perfect mastery of magic allowed them to establish communication between the living and the dead. They were especially feared for their ability to manipulate evil forces to cast spells.

Later, all these secrets and magic recipes were brought together into a mystical theory, strongly influenced by cultural contributions from India and the neighboring countries. In the kingdom of Shangshung in the 11th century, a school of *Bonpo*, desirous of keeping its distance from fast-spreading Buddhism, gained status by being recognized as a religion in its own right. Its influence was so great that it has survived until today and some of its rites can be found in the doctrine of *Nyingmapa*, the oldest Buddhist school in Tibet.

Although *Bonpo* and Buddhism have been ruthless foes and, in the 9th century, their rivalry caused the collapse of the Tibetan kingdom, these two religions have never been fundamentally antagonistic, simply because they were the two parallel currents of the same doctrine. Indeed, it was not difficult for Vajrayanic thought to absorb a large part of the *bonpo* heritage. The latter, like the Diamond Vehicle, conceives the universe as three worlds one superposed on another: the upper, inhabited by gods and good spirits and associated with snow-capped mountains, the middle, where men and animals live ("mystical bridges" including physical transformations were possible between them), and the lower world, peopled with evil genies and spirits and a multitude of monsters. The latter are closely related o the *rakshasa* (man-eating demons), *raktapa* (blood-drinking genies), *matangi* (lost women), *pishaci* (succubi) and other *dakini* (vampires) of Mayanic and Tantric Buddhism. The *bon* magician priests were shamans responsible for preserving the unstable order of the universe. Like them, the first Buddhist priests sought to master the Upper World and the Lower World esoterically. *Bon*, like Buddhism, erected monasteries, temples and established schools to reinforce its popular basis. Finally, the Master Shenrab very much resembles the Buddha Shakyamuni.

So, at the present time, there is a tendency to regard *Bon* as an original and early attempt within the Buddhist movement. Buddhism cannot be seriously studied while disregarding *Bon* which must be considered an authentic Buddhist sect. After numerous political and religious crises which often degenerated into violent confrontations, *Vajrayana*, which originated in India, has progressively absorbed important elements of native *Bon* and given rise to an original form of Buddhism, known as Lamaism, or Tibetan Buddhism.

The popular basis of Lamaism is such that the faith completely blended with Tibetan culture. The Tibetans have no word for "Buddhist". They use instead the word *nangpa*, which designates the "insiders", that is, themselves, as opposed to the *phyipa*, "the outsiders", or foreigners, actually the non-Buddhists. For centuries, the Tibetans were the subjects of a theocratic aristocracy and they gradually came to consider themselves a chosen people, set apart by the various Buddhas and *Bodhisattva* to receive their revelations and teachings.

Undoubtedly, this religious narcissism accounts for the often proud and patronizing attitude of the Tibetans who looked down upon other cultures and who, even today, despite the very positive image given by their pacifist and tolerant attitude, regard their spiritual culture as far more advanced than the other religions.

The Lamaist Schools

The Tibetan region remained isolated from all forms of Buddhism until the end of the 2nd century BC. In the previous century, Hinayanist missionaries, sent by the emperor Ashoka to Nepal and Ladakh, had vainly tried to enter Tibet itself. However, they paved the way for other saintly men, this time belonging to *Mahayana* who, coming from Nepal and central China, succeeded in their endeavors a century later. And yet, it was only in 640 AD that Buddhism officially entered Tibet. That year, King Songtsen Gampo, after marrying two Buddhist princesses, one from Nepal, the other from China, officially converted to the new faith, which then became the official religion.

Three other people were to organize the introduction of the new religion in Tibet and to be directly or indirectly responsible for all Lamaist schools.

In 750, an Indian *mahasiddha* ("great master") was summoned by King Trisong Detsen to conciliate Buddhist canon and *bonpo* cults. He was the famous Padmasambhava ("Born in a lotus bud") who became the revered and feared patriarch of Lamaism under the name of Guru Rinpoche. He founded the school of the *Nyingmapa* or "Lineage of the Ancients". In order to differentiate themselves from the *bonpo* clergy always dressed in black robes and hats, his monks started wearing red robes and hats, hence their name "Red Hats". Nowadays, this school distinguishes two types of spiritual quest: that of the monks, adepts of a

Mani are prayer stones which are laid down on special outdoor walls and altars, the manidong *(or* mendong)*. These flat stones are engraved and painted with votive formulas, namely the famous* Chenrezi *mantra "Om mane padme hum."*

It is customary in Tibet for the main roads to be marked by religious symbols and paintings. This huge painting is along the main road from Gonggar to Lhasa.

Monks belonging to the
Kagyupa school of the
"Yellow Hats" are praying
in the courtyard of one of
the Bodnath monasteries.

Some young postulants
having fun turning the
prayer wheels that surround
the outside wall of the
Labrang temple. Before
going inside, believers
circle the building clockwise,
turning the prayer wheels
which "say for them"
all the sacred formulas
contained within them.

communal life, and that of the *yogi*, who have chosen the solitary way.

The 10th and 11th centuries were crucial in the consolidation of Buddhism which had recently been endangered by Langdarma, in Tibet. In India, Tilopa, the most famous of the *mahasiddha*, was the first of a long unbroken line of contemplative *yogi*. All the

One of the head abbots watching over novices studying in one of the Tsurpshu prayer rooms. This sanctuary is particularly venerated by the followers of the Karmapa school, because it is home to the young boy who is the most recent reincarnation of the Karmapa.

Lamaist schools, called semi-reformed to differentiate them from the *Nyingmapa*, which were about to come into existence, were directly or indirectly inspired by his teachings that were propagated by his main disciple, Naropa, the abbot-director of the Buddhist university of Nalanda. Their pupils or other masters greatly influenced by their doctrine, came to Tibet. One of the most important was Atisha (Dorje Paldan in Tibetan), mandated to revitalize Buddhism, which was threatened by the revival of *Bonpo*. One of his disciples, Domton (or Bromston) founded the *Kadampa* sect, the "Lineage of Oral Transmission", on which the *Gelugpa* sect was later based.

Other disciples, Tibetan this time, of the Tilopa-Naropa lineage, founded major sects. Brogmi created the *Sakyapa* sect ("Lineage of the Grey Earth") while Rechung Respa and Gampopa (students of Milarespa who had himself received the teachings of Marpa) founded the *Kagyupa* sect ("Lineage of Oral Transmission"), which later subdivided into *Karma kagyu*, *Tsalpa kagyu*, *Baram kagyu*, *Phagmo drugpa kagyu*. The monks belonging to all these schools were referred to

Along with the clergy who live in lamasaries and temples, there are many itinerant monks who go from shrine to shrine at the holidays. This old man is turning his prayer wheel at the entrance to Sera in Lhasa.

 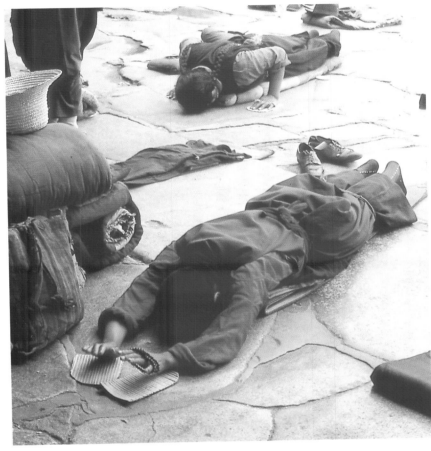

The khenpo (*head abbot*) from Lundup Gansel, a gelupka monastery founded
in Kanun in the 13th century. The habit, the liturgical form
and the placing of the cult objects are quite original, for Kinnaur, although
a Tibetan fief for a long time, has developed its own rites.

In order to obtain favors from a god or to be forgiven a fault, the faithful
recite their prayers along with a long series of prostrations at the entrance
to Jokhang, the most venerated Tibetan sanctuary.

as Red Hats, but some were called Black Hats, to distinguish them from the *Nyingmapa*, such as the *Karmapa* which, in the 12th century, invented the idea of the successive reincarnations of a same person, a notion later taken up by all sects.

Around 1400 the event which established Lamaism as the dominant religion in Tibet occurred. A great Tibetan reformer called Tsongkhapa ("Born in the country of onions"), later named Je Rinpoche ("Most Precious Lightning Diamond"), appeared in the region of Kumbum. Versed in the *sakyapa* doctrine, he decided to start from the tenets of the *kadampa* school and to gather the essence of all known Buddhist teachings into a single canon which he entrusted to a new expressly created school, the *Gelugpa* ("The Virtuous"). Its members adopted the yellow robe and the yellow hat and were consequently called "Yellow Hats". His nephew, Gedun Truppa (or Gedungdub) became the spiritual leader of the *Gelugpa*, then the temporal guide of Tibet, initiating the lineage of the future Dalai Lamas.

In 1650, the third sovereign-god of Tibet, Sonam Gyatso, received from a Mongol king the title of Dalai Lama, meaning "Ocean of Wisdom" which was retrospectively applied to his four predecessors. From that time on, each Dalai Lama was considered the reincarnation of his predecessor. To this day, fourteen "Oceans" have succeeded one another. The fourteenth, recognized as the chief-god of all the schools of the Tibetan community, cannot, as custom would have it, reside in the Potala at Lhasa, having had to flee the Chinese occupation and to seek refuge in Dharamsala, India. Besides the Dalai Lama, who is endowed with moral and secular authority, the Lamaist hierarchy has another high dignitary, the Panchen Lama ("Great Learned One") whose function was defined in the 17th century by the fifth Dalai Lama. Also considered the reincarnation of the former Panchen Lama, he has no hold on the external world and dedicates himself entirely to spiritual matters. In the course of centuries, Panchen Lamas, often regarded as more "saintly", because less in contact with temporal matters, than Dalai Lamas, rebelled against the latter. Their seat is the great monastery of Tashilunpo. The present, and tenth, Panchen Lama, has left Tibet and now works in Beijing.

Dance of wrathful deities and demons in a small temple near Tsedang.
These formidable entities are the center of complex cults whose constant aim
is to calm them. They were inherited from the bonpo religion and have become
the sensitive protectors of the Buddhist faith.

The temples are closed at night and certain hours of the day. The faithful wait
patiently for the doors to open in order to worship the sacred effigies or simply
to see the cult objects that the monks transport before each service.

These long telescopic horns, which give forth a strange hoarse sound
are called radung. They can be up to three meters in length. Long ago
they were used to communicate from one valley to another. They have
since been integrated into Buddhist ritual.

Collective prayer of the gelugpa monks belonging to the first Tantric college of
the Tashilunpo monastery in Shigatse. In the past, over 4,000 monks belonged
to the four colleges of the monastery. Despite the ravages of the Cultural
Revolution, there are approximately 700 of them today, including 130 novices.

A tsabai lama, "*root-abbot*", in Drepung is looking in the holy books for something to teach. When he has found the right passages, he will comment on them with his peers before proposing them to his pupils for study.

Gyangtse monks collectively reading the Kangyur (*one of the two encyclopedias of Buddhism*) under the iron rule of two lama masters in a prayer room of the Palkhor monastery (Baiju).

Buddhism has no women monks. It does, however, admit to its religious
communities, convents of nuns, governed by the lamas. Two nuns frying
wheat patties in the Kanun monastery in Kinnaur.

This monk is the cook at the Drigungtil monastery and is preparing
the evening meal. As one can see, not all monasteries have the same status
and the same wealth! On the left stands the high-cyclindered churn
in which the tea with salted butter is prepared.

On a cool spring morning, several monks from the Ralung monastery are having their daily cup of tea mixed with tsampa. The monastery is located at an altitude of 16,400 feet and is the main sanctuary of the Drugpa school in Tibet.

Two novices from the Tashilhunpo monastery in Shigatse taking cow's milk to the monastery kitchen. They are responsible for all the domestic tasks, as are all the other young men who have not yet been confirmed as gelong (monks).

Big beams are used to make the roofs sturdy. Tibetan artists have taken advantage of what could have been an esthetic handicap by extending the ridge beams and by decorating them with brightly colored traditional motives. They have made them into a first-class decorative element.

The geographical location of the Tibetan expanse at the crossroads of four great realms of artistic creation, China, India, Kashmir, Nepal –all thousands of years old– has given Tibetan art exceptionally rich "materials" that its own genius has progressively fashioned into one of the world's most original arts.

Tibetan art has two main characteristics. Its subjects are almost always religious, as in all countries where Buddhism has become a major force, and it is very conservative, in as much as the artists faithfully return to the centuries-old themes and archetypes of their predecessors. But the embodiment of the Tibetan creative spirit, however, derives from the fact that each school has added its own personal touch. There are approximately three hundred schools, which explains the surprising variety in Tibetan esthetic expression. All of them have best illustrated their skills in statues and in painting.

Statuary art

The Tibetan artists are past masters at working those metals that abound in their region, namely copper, which is widespread, as well as silver and gold, of which large deposits are found in the Khams and the Amdo. There is also iron, lead, zinc and to a lesser extent, tin. If a given metal becomes scarce, the Tibetans continue, as they have done for centuries, to import it from Nepal, India or China.

Copper is the main element used in the making of bronze in which most of the statues are cast, according to a technique dating back to the 9th century at least. Starting from an original form carefully sculpted in wood, and only rarely in soft stone, a terra cotta mold is made; for small or medium-sized objects molds are made of wax, which is then discarded. For large statues the repoussé method is used on malleable metals (silver or native gold). The various pieces are then soldered or riveted together.

The influence of foreign artists –Indians, Nepalese (especially the Nevari) and Chinese– is omnipresent. The Indian esthetic standards are easily recognizable, for instance, in the way the wide, rounded shoulders are rendered, as well as the very conspicuous and delineated abdominals and pectorals, so characteristic of the Buddhist artists of Gandhara (from eastern Afghanistan to northwestern Pakistan) or Kashmir. Another Indian touch, most likely of Pala origin, can be found in the frequent use of ungilded bronze, occasionally set in various alloys.

Tibetan art

The Nepalese influence appears in the constant association of gold and silver with bronze, producing a subtle play of colors, particularly in gold leaf or mercury gilded statues. Often some are enhanced with gold or silver-plating in order to emphasize the folds in the clothing, or with precious stones or pearls set in diadems, necklaces or bracelets.

Chinese art has always had a predilection for colossal, an influence reflected in Tibetan art since the 10th century. At that time they began to build gigantic statues of Buddha, the Bodhisattva and other Tara. Simultaneously, monastery and temple roofs were adorned with huge animals inspired by Chinese mythology (dragons, open-mouthed makara, contorted evil or friendly spirits) and their own Buddhist symbols (Wheels of Life, Wheels of Law, conch shells, umbrellas and finials).

Clay statuary also is widespread in the southern shrines (Narthang, Rinbung, Sakya and Shalu). There is a minor, but very active tradition of wooden statuary in western Tibet (Luk, Tsaparang), which was directly inspired by Kashmiri artists, and several schools of stone sculpture in the round (Shalu, Mangnang), either miniatures or bas-reliefs on the mountain sides.

Besides the statues, as such, sculptural art is also evident in the prayer stones, covered with mantra, and piled up on the walls (mani dong or mendong) close to the shrines or along the pilgrims' walks. Some of these walls may be several hundred yards long, particularly in Ladakh.

Various other cultural objects also allow the artists to display their talents. Most common are the finely engraved vajra (dorje in Tibetan) and ghanta (rilbu in Tibetan) which are often enhanced with stones and precious metals. When they are brought together during a religious service, they represent the intimate union of the material and the spiritual, the masculine and the feminine worlds, as the Tantric rites require. The vajra, held in the officiant's right hand symbolizes the diamond thunderbolt; it consists of a short bronze axis, both sides of which end in a point around which are united two, four, six, or eight other blunt spikes. This symbol originated in Brahmanic mythology, which considered it the unfailing "thousand-pointed" missile of the god Indra, and represents in Tibet the radiance of the Spirit which has freed itself of all material appearances and contingencies. The gantha is held in his left hand; its rhythmic ringing during the incantation of the mantra is said to drive away evil influences.

The prayer wheel (mani khorlo) deserves separate mention. It is the fetish of Tibetan Buddhists who will unhesitatingly pay great sums for it to be beautifully engraved and decorated. The prayer wheel consists of a cylinder containing one or several rolls of paper inscribed with sacred formulas and it rotates in a clockwise fashion. There are two sorts of prayer wheels:

one is small and personal, and is attached to a wooden handle that the worshipper holds in his right hand; the second, a huge prayer wheel, rotates on a fixed axis and can be found in niches or in a room reserved for it in the entrance to a shrine. Long rows of smaller prayer wheels line the outside walls of monasteries and temples so that the worshippers can set them in

artists found their style, but before that time they were strongly influenced by contributions from Indian, Nepalese and Chinese art. In the 10th and 11th centuries, the Tibetan armies which had just invaded the southwest territories, came into contact with the Indo-European populations, particularly the Kashmiris, who had created a very elaborate art form. The

The wheel of the Law (Thabdong Shesrab) *is placed on the roof of the temple entrance. It represents Buddha and the dance of rebirth. The two deer on each side symbolize the first disciples of Buddha.*

motion as they make the ritual circumambulation of the buildings. Whatever their size, the prayer wheels serve the same function: to repeat the holy formulas for the faithful who are busy doing other tasks and do not have time to recite the *mantra*. One must not forget that systematical repetition of the sacred formulas is the surest guarantee of attaining salvation. And by means of a prayer wheel they are repeated ad infinitum! A simple personal prayer wheel contains one hundred pages. The Avalokiteshvara *mantra* (Chenrezi in Tibetan) is written four thousand times on each page. Therefore, one single rotation of the cylinder "recites" four hundred thousand prayers !

Painting

The most complete expression of the Tibetan soul is found in its painting, the art form best known to the outside world. Sacred Tibetan paintings are omnipresent in the streets, on rock faces, on the facades of houses, as well as in monasteries and temples. They are found on any number of supports, from paper on which the sacred formulas and symbols are drawn, to the broad walls of the shrines covered with *mandala* or huge frescoes, to the cloth used for the prayer flags or the linen of the *thangka*. By the 14th century, Tibetan

Tibetans adopted their way of dividing space into squares, the ascetic postures of their human figures with their typical loose-fitting clothes, and their use of bright colors. The 14th century bears the stamp of the brief but important Iranian influence which left its imprint on Tibetan pictoral concepts. Drawing inspiration from Persian miniatures, Tibetan art multiplied the number of tiny scenes within one painting and meticulously emphasized the detailed precision of each scene. Starting in the 15th century, three rival tendencies profoundly modified the Tibetan spirit. One came from China, the second from central Asia and the last from Nepal. From the Chinese, the Tibetans adopted the themes of horses, cavalcades and parades. From the non-Chinese Asians, the carefully folded, decorated tunics. Lastly, from the Nepalese, the hieratic majesty and the refined elegance of the human figures. After being enriched by all these cultures, Tibetan painting then gave free rein to its originality; its most characteristic feature was the desire to be accessible to the masses. Although originally conceived as decoration for the buildings of an aristocratic, theocratic society, Tibetan art always sought to seduce, convince and strengthen the faith of the common man who found in the paintings and drawings the same lessons

One of the other temples of the Thiksey monastery in Ladakh has a huge statue
of Maitreya, the next Manushi Buddha. This bodhisattva of goodness
who still lives in the "Paradise of the Satisfied" is supposed to become
incarnate on earth at the end of the present cycle.

that life and tradition taught and repeated to him daily.

There are two types of Tibetan painting: figurative and abstract. Examples of the former are the murals previously mentioned and the *thangka*. *Thangka* means "plain" or " object that is unfurled". They are, in fact, painted on cloth and hung from private homes, as well as temples and monasteries, where they constitute veritable colored aerial galeries. The *thangka* depict traditional figures and themes. They are framed by three strips of blue, yellow and red material evoking the halo of the saint or the god they portray. Another piece of ornate material inlaid at the bottom symbolizes the mystic "gateway" to the invisible world. Some *thangka* are embroidered and few are more than three feet long. Nevertheless, there are some very large ones called *goku* kept in monasteries, such as the one in the Potala in Lhasa, which is 184 feet by 154 feet. They are taken out on exceptional ceremonial occasions. The Tibetans have several different schools of *thangka*. The most famous are the Manri strongly influenced by the Chinese (beginning of the 15th century), the more detailed Khyenri (15-16th century), the shining, bright-colored Byuri (16th century) and the neo-Manri, that syncretize the earlier forms that most contemporary artists have adopted.

There are numerous subjects of the figurative painting. They tell of episodes from the lives of different Buddhas and *Bodhisattva* and their consorts, depicting them either as compassionate or wrathful. They also present the vast pantheon of beneficent or evil gods, particularly the four *loka pala* (in Tibetan *jigten kyong*) the guardins of the four directions of the world, the *Dharma pala* (in Tibetan *chokyong*) the guardians of Buddhist Law, often presented in their terrifying form, the *heruka* (in Tibetan *palchenpo*), irate gods that personify the masculine Buddhist qualities, and the *dakini* (in Tibetan *khadoma*), which symbolize the feminine Buddhist qualities, not to mention the host of saints and historical figures, such as Padmasambhava (Padma Jungna in Tibetan), Nagarjuna (Ludup in Tibetan), Atisha (Jovove in Tibetan), Milarespa, Tsongkhapa, Songstsen Gampo, Bhrikuti (Tritsum in Tibetan), Wengcheng (Kongio in Tibetan) and the Dalai and Panchen Lamas.

There is one particular motif, commonly found on monastery walls, that foreigners know and appreciate for its almost rational symbolism: the *bhavachakra* (*sidpa khorlo* in Tibetan) or Wheel of Life. Held within the claws of the Mahakala (*Gonpo* in Tibetan), "The Universal Time", this mystic wheel is composed of four concentric circles which depict, starting from the center, the "three poisons", the contradictory movements that draw people towards happiness or unhappiness, six realms of possible reincarnation, and the twelve successive causes of existence.

The Buddhist shrines in Kinnaur are protected by animals that defend their entrances. In accordance with the local artistic custom, sculptures are never made of stone, but of wood, decorated with metal.

Tibetan statuary adopted ancient Bonpo themes and adapted them to the Buddhist tradition. After assimilating subsequent Nepalese and Chinese techniques, it produced exceptional Lamaist art as early as the 15th century.

The bronze statues are often completely gilded or enhanced ▶ by gold or silver plating. Combined with the use of precious stones, these two valuable metals are used to emphasize the folds of the clothing or the deities' jewelry and ornaments.

The palette of the traditional abstract painting is not so broad, but undoubtedly concentrates more on superstitious respect and fervor than the figurative paintings do. The most typical are the *mandala* (*kyil-kor* in Tibetan) and the *bija* (*saben* in Tibetan) which are often associated. A *mandala* is a geometrical diagram representing the cosmic order. It serves as the archi-

"descends" along the central axis so that the faithful can blend into the god. The five cardinal points (the four "gateways" and the central zenith) then become the seat of the five Dhyani Buddha that the five colors and the five *bija* evoke. During ritual initiations or to protect a home, temporary *mandala* may be drawn of the ground with colored powders.

tectural pattern for a *chorten*, for a temple or some-times even for an offering. The *bija* or "kernel syllable" is a sound which, by its vibrations, is supposed to arouse the deity it symbolizes.

The *mandala* represents the fundamental structure of the universe as seen in two dimensions and is gene-rally oriented west east, according to the Buddhist geographical tradition. It is drawn as a double circle, or sometimes several circles, around a central focal point representing the axis of the world. Beyond the outer circle, usually inscribed in a square, are four symetrically located "gateways" that lead to the four main continents.

From an esoteric point of view, the *mandala* become a symbol for meditation, when the god who is invoked

In addition to these major symbols there is a whole series of abstract representations which are very im-portant in Buddhist liturgy: the endless knot (*apalbe*) that signifies the unity of all things and the illusory character of time, the *svastika* (*gyung drung* in Tibetan) that brings good fortune, the diagram of the sun and the moon together, which wards off evil spirits, the *kalachakra mantra* (usually painted in the vestibules) that expresses the highest of all initiations into occult knowledge which can only be performed by a Dalai Lama.

The subject of Tibetan painting is always religious. It most often depicts scenes
representing the life of Buddha, the bodhisattva and various divinities
taken from Buddhist dogma or the pantheon . Even when secular scenes are shown,
such as a king's court or a hermit's life, they are always related to historical events
which glorify a very religious sovereign or a particularly deserving ascetic.

*Whereas the Chinese influence is evident in the two paintings on the preceding
pages, the subjects presented above, as well as the techniques used,
reveal clear* Bonpo *and* Hinduist *contributions.*

IV

The eastern Himalayas

from Sikkim and Bhutan to Arunachal Pradesh

The eastern Himalayas are located at a lower latitude than the rest of the chain. In addition, their general orientation is not northwest southeast as elsewhere, but west northeast, which has it perpendicularly facing the monsoon winds. These two factors mean that from March to September the valley bottoms are subject to an exceptional assault of tropical precipitation which may exceed 157 inches, but is never lower than an average of 110 inches. This also explains both the level of the permanent snowline (above 18,000 feet) and the almost total absence of glaciers, except in the close vicinity of certain of the highest peaks. There are numerous microclimates due to the steep valleys that are increasingly humid as one goes eastward. Most of the eastern Himalayas consist of large overthrust nappes, wrinkled and ruptured at the orogeny of the chain. As a result , the precipitous, hostile appearance of the impressive massifs is accentuated as one approaches the Chinese Longmanshan fold.

The rhododendron is the symbol of the eastern Himalayas. In the springtime, the mountain slopes are studded with the many hues of flowering rhododendrons. These deciduous or coriaceous trees and bushes bear bouquets or corymb flowers whose bell-shaped corollas or infundibula have from five to ten lobes. They grow in acidic soils (pH between 4 and 5). Their flowering cycle takes place as the days grow longer and when night temperatures are not below 6°C. The spangled mountainside display found here is unique. Without going into fastidious detail concerning the species, it, nevertheless, seems worthwhile to point out some of the most beautiful specimens encountered in this region.

Of all the colors, red is the one which attracts and retains one's eye. Although there is a broad variety of hues, the most beautiful rhododendrons are blood red or dark red. Some that deserve special mention are: the *arboreum*, whose flowers have a delicately serrated corolla, the *barbatum*, whose bell-shaped flowers bear very dark crimson spots at their base, the *cinnabarium*, easily recognizable by its bell-mouthed corollas, or the *fulgens* with its long chocolate-colored anthers, and the large-flowered *thomsonii*. The tints of magenta and violet are often associated with pink and these species, too, are superb. Among the most arresting are the *setosum* with deep infundibulate flowers and long stymens, the lavender-colored *nivale* that prefer dry ground, the pale violet *virgatum*, one of the rare species to bear single or double axillary flowers, and the *campanulatum* whose bark and leaves have medicinal properties.

IV
The eastern Himalayas: from Sikkim and Bhutan to Arunachal Pradesh

A *garden of rhododendrons*

Among the numerous varieties of pink rhododendrons are the *hodgsonii* whose flowers come in long corymbs, the *pumilum*, whose flowers dangle at the end of their long stems, the *vaccinioides*, which, on the contrary, have tiny pink-tipped white or pink flowers, the large-flowered *ciliatum*, whose corolla turns to white towards the top, and the *glaucophyllum*, with their small white flowers speckled with red or pink dots.

The yellows constantly vacillate between tones of pale pink and pale green. The most common species are the *lanatum*, of which the pale yellow interior of the corolla is dotted with tiny red spots, the *campylocarpum* with crimson specks at their base, the *falconeri* and their pale violet interior, the *trichocladum*, with dark green spotted flowers, and some particularly fragrant varieties with pale yellow flowers spotted and dotted with green (*triflorum*) or pink (*anthropogon*) on the outside or crimson on the inside (*wightii*, *lanatum*) and the *dalhousiae*, which has an interesting story. The English botanist, Hooker, who was exploring Sikkim between 1848 and 1850 (where he inventoried twenty-two new species), discovered this rhododendron which he named *dalhousiae* in honor of Lady Dalhousie, the wife of the Governor General at the time.

The white rhododendrons are often cream-colored. One finds magnificent specimens of the pink-veined *cameliiflorum*, the *grande* whose rose tinted flowers appear in bouquets, the *griffithianum* and the *lindleyi* with their large, perfumed flowers.

We are still far from knowing all the rhododendrons; every year new discoveries are made.

◄ *Rhododendrons bloom in the spring. The large-flowered arborescent varieties grow at altitudes between 9,200 and 9,800 feet. In these humid misty areas their branches are often covered with hanging lichens. The dwarf species growing above this elevation are bushes with smaller flowers.*

Originating in the freezing mountain heights, the Tista rushes southward,
swollen by its many tributaries. It becomes a wide river, winding through
coniferous and oak forests, before arriving in the Terai lowlands.

Sikkim signifies "happy land", an appellation given it during the Middle Ages by Tibetan princes astounded by the lush natural beauty that was such a change from their arid land. Throughout its history, Sikkim has suffered numerous disappointments. A large part of the Lepcha and Tsong territories to the east was lost, having been seized by the Nepalese Gurkhas. In the 19th century, the British East India Company annexed the Darjeeling district and the lowlands of the south, while Tibet annexed the northern valleys and Bhutan took those to the east. Finally, after several disputes with the Indian government concerned about protecting its Himalayan borders against surprise attack from the Chinese, the King of Sikkim was overthrown and the country joined the Indian Union, thereby, becoming one of the twenty-two states. The early inhabitants were the Lepcha, Tibeto-Burmese who had migrated from the east or mixed with less well-identified indigenous peoples. When the first Tibetans, grouped around a princely family of the Namgyal clan, arrived in Sikkim in the 13th century, they composed a "bhotia" nucleus. This Anglo-Indian term comes from the sanskrit *Bod*, meaning "Tibet", and designates all the Tibetan peoples living outside Tibet on the southern slopes of the Himalayas. Later the Nepalese and then the Indians arrived in Sikkim and the latter now are the predominant ethnic group of the country. Their growing presence has pushed the Tibetan populations to the northern regions of the country and has had a profound influence of the political life of Sikkim.

However, if Sikkim exists, it is not due to the people that inhabit it, but to the great river, the Tista, that flows through it. This waterway originates in the Tista, one of the rare glaciers of the eastern Himalayas. After sweeping westward, it heads south, swollen with the waters of its tributaries, the Zemu from the west and the Lachung, also snow-fed from the Tista glacier. The Rangpo and the Talung discharge on its left and right banks, respectively, before the Tista drops 8,200 feet in 43 miles to the Indian piedmont where the Rangit joins it. Further along it crosses the tropical forest and empties into the Brahmaputra. This exceptional hydrographic network is what created Sikkim. These waterways have dug through soft ground in the center, sparing the hard metamorphic rocks which are the natural surroundings of the country. The final result is an

One river shapes Sikkim

immense amphitheater turning its back to the Great Himalayas which isolate it from Tibet and bordered by the two powerful Sangalila and Chola ranges. The massive Kanchenjunga (28,208 feet) in the Sangalila range is the highest peak and separates Sikkim from Nepal to the west; the Chola, to the east delimits the boundary with Bhutan.

The very shape of Sikkim fosters the abundant monsoons that the high summits retain, thus developing lush tropical vegetation in the lowlands, then giving rise to temperate forests as one climbs higher in the valleys. From June to September the Tista and its tributaries become tempestuous rivers which will provide great quantities of hydro-electric power once the projected dams have been built. During the rest of the year these rivers ensure the normal irrigation of the valleys.

Some of the upper reaches of the waterways played a considerable role in settling the country, acting, over the centuries, as natural axes for migration between the Tibetan plateau and the Bengali plain. Caravans followed them both up and downstream, ensuring, until the mid-twentieth century, a flourishing trade that crossed the Himalayan passes at over 16,400 feet. These rivers also conveyed incredible amounts of alluviums and materials that were left in their middle and lower courses where they formed easily-farmed fertile lands. This is where the majority of the population lives, at an altitude of between 900 and 7,200 feet. Farmers, especially Nepalese, Indians and Bengalis pursue intensive farming that brings in biannual harvests of high-altitude rice, different varieties of millet, corn, wheat and fruit from the terraced orchards along the valley slopes. The high glacial valleys of the north are home to scattered populations of Tibetan origin. They are poor and earn their livelihood from subsistence, often itinerant, farming and cow and sheep raising.

As is the case in most eastern Himalayan countries, Sikkim has been subjected to a heavy migratory flow of the Nepalese diaspora. The emigrants gather in certain areas of the country where, in the end, they constitute the majority of the population and rapidly give voice to autonomist claims. This is so for the Gurkhas who settled in the west and radically changed the face of the country. They cleared almost all the land in the hot temperate belt, between 4,000 and

6,500 feet, creating enormous friction with their neighbors who accused them of destroying the forest.

Once again, it may be thanks to the Tista and its network of tributaries that the authentic Sikkimese culture owes its survival. The Lepchas and the Bhotias who retreated to the highlands have kept in contact with Tibet and Bhutan via trade and cultural relations which continue to exist along the waterways. If by some fluke of politics, relations with the north and east were to be cut off, there is no doubt that the Sikkimese civilization would become extinct, blocked off as it is to the south by the masses of Indianized inhabitants. But for this to happen, one side must control all of the passages in the large and small Himalayan rivers valleys; even during the Sino-Indian conflict in 1962 neither side was able to do it. As long as the Tista flows, Sikkim is likely to exist.

Typical landscape of middle Sikkim with its network of terraced ricefields emerging from lush vegetation. The photograph of this hamlet, situated along the Gangtok, was taken in June just after the first monsoons brighten nature's colors.

A great many immigrants, coming essentially from neighboring Nepal and looking for arable land, continue to settle along the rivers and main roads where they live cut off from the Sikkimese.

The famous Rumtek monastery before it was restored. It harbors the biggest
monastic community of Sikkim and is governed by Gyalwa Karmapa, head
of the kagyupa school (profound vision), which was inspired by the
"Great Wiseman", Milarepa, who lived in the 11th century.

*The monastery pictured above as it is today. Many secondary buildings
(chapels, temples, monks cells) and new pilgrims' walks, lined with prayer flags,
have been constructed around the original monastery.*

Even the most humble monastery has a library. It is generally located
in the dukhang (prayer room) where the manuscripts and two encyclopedias of
Buddhism, the Kangyur and the Tangyur, are kept.

The valley bottoms in the middle mountain belt
(here, the Sankosh River valley) are lined with intensively farmed
terraces that grow rice below and barley above 4,900 feet.

Bhutan is a fascinating small kingdom that climbs from the valleys of the Duars and is separated from the Tibetan plateau by a line of lofty peaks. With the exception of the hills to the south, that represent only 5% of its territory and whose tropical climate is a continuation of the Nepalese Terai, Bhutan is entirely composed of the ranges of the Lesser and the Great Himalayas. The Lesser Himalayas' elevation is generally not greater that 10,500 feet, although the Black Mountain Range reaches 17,963 feet. The average elevation of the Great Himalayas, on the other hand, varies between 16,500 and 19,700 feet, with several peaks over 23,000 feet, including Chomolhari (23,996 feet) and Kula Khangri (24,948 feet). As in neighboring Sikkim, many north south valleys formed by water running off the Himalayan peaks and cutting through mountains have divided the country into isolated basins. This unusual geographical situation has fostered, in the valleys between 3,900 and 8,200 feet of altitude, distinct cultures that make Bhutan so original. The Bhutanese call their kingdom Drug Yul, the "Land of the Dragon" and call themselves the Grugpa or the "People of the Dragon". The region had been previously known as Lho Yul ("Land of the Southern Valleys") or Mon Yul ("Land of the Mon", that is, non-Tibetans) or by other such poetic appellations as Lho-mon Kashi ("Land of the Southern Valleys with Four Entrances Inhabited by the Mon"), or Lhojong Menjong ("Land of the Southern Valleys with Medicinal Herbs and Inhabited by the Mon). According to a legend, at the end of the 11th century, Buddhist monks, disciples of Tsangpa Gyare, arrived here. Tsangpa Gyare had founded the Drug monastery in central Tibet after hearing a violent clap of thunder that the natives likened to the clamor of a celestial dragon (pronounced *drug* in Tibetan). Later, in the 17th century, when the Europeans began to take an interest in Tibet, the first natural obstacle along their way was the Land of the Dragon which they described in their notes as "The first state of Potente" (the anglicized form of the Indian word *bhotanta*, meaning all the territories on Tibet's southern border). This word soon became Bhutan.

A feudal society

Of all the Himalayan states, Bhutan has always known best how to protect itself from outside influences. Even today, the number of tourists allowed to visit the country is strictly limited. Under the rule of the sovereigns of the Wangchuck dynasty, and particularly that of the current king, Jigme Singye, and his father, Bhutan has kept its feudal-type society based on *drugpa* Lamaism quite intact. This school of thought, which adopts the basic doctrine of *kagyupa*, emphasizes the *Mahamudra* (*Chagya Chenpo* in Tibetan) or "Great Attitude". Accordingly, by uniting the passive

Bhutan, the kingdom of the dragon

female principle and the active male principle through meditation, one reaches knowledge and attains ultimate wisdom, or consciousness of the emptiness of a world dominated by illusion.

The kingdom perpetuates one of the oldest cultures of the Himalayas, very likely dating back to the early Tibetan migrations before the Christian era. Their descendants congregated in the eastern part of the country where they were called Sharchop, in opposition to Ngalop, who descended from later Tibetan migrations, especially from the 8th to 12th centuries. The theocratic Tibetan tradition found fertile ground in Bhutan, where warlords had always been the dominant class. When the system collapsed in Tibet, it survived here. There are, thus, three clearly differentiated social classes. At the top are the few great noble clans, mainly descendants of the Tibetans who came to Bhutan during the Middle Ages. Isolated in their proud solitude, these aristocrats, whose ancestors were legendary heroes, take little part in public affaires. Most of them live in the central and eastern parts of the country. On the other hand, a few noble families in the west are more open to the modern world and play a prominent role in politics. They –the Dorje of the Ha valley and the Nyos of Bhumtang (from whom the current ruling family descends)– generally claim kinship with Buddhist saints. Besides the nobles, there is a large class of clergy. Members of religious communities, often of aristocratic descent, play an important part in the political life. The *jekhenpo*, the chief spiritual authority, alone can designate the king. The country is governed from *zong* (monastery-fortresses) which relay governmental decisions. Finally, the last, or plebeian class, consists of a number of subclasses ranging from the solid middle class, via lowly civil servants and artisans, to humble farmers. The peasants compose over 90% of the population of Bhutanese origin. They are profoundly religious people who venerate the royal family and scrupulously respect traditions.

There is one phenomenon, however, which is unique among Buddhist countries: the masses of people who are not part of this social pyramid. Their status cannot be compared with that of the Hindu untouchables, because these "associated" populations, to use the official term, enjoy rights they would never have in the Hindu system.

Nevertheless, the condition of the Nepalese, Bengali, Bihari and other Assamese immigrants is hardly enviable; they are looked down upon and generally confined to the tropical zones. All the lowly tasks and hardest jobs are left for them, such as the upkeep of the "100,000 bends of the celestial way", a vertiginous road that crosses the country from west to east along which they live in miserable shacks of branches and sheet metal. Finally, at the bottom of the social ladder, one finds the strange group of *zapa* ("workers"), state slaves, descendants of prisoners of war, and the *trapa* ("free peasants"). Slavery was abolished in Bhutan in 1964, but the *zapa* still remain the dregs of society in the eyes of the old Bhutanese families and the *trapa* continue to cultivate monastic lands and to pay taxes in kind.

When temporal and spiritual power concord

The feudal system also appears in the network of *zong*, of Tibetan origin, but perfected in Bhutan. A *zong* is a monastery-fortress whose original function was to exert military and economic control over a valley. Today the *zong* house civil servants and large monastic communities. The latter perpetuate the strict Buddhist tradition and foster remarkable art schools. The most renowned are, in the west, the Paro and Punakha *zong* (where the *jekhenpo* has his offices); those of Tongsa and Byakar in the center, and those of Mongar and Lhuntsi in the eastern part of the country. Many novices and monks come here to learn the arts from distinguished masters who perpetuate the canons of the classical tradition.

The *zong* are the administrative backbone of the country. Bhutan is divided into eighteen *zongkhag*, districts depending directly on the Ministry of the Interior, each administered by one of the country's thirty-two *zong*. They are jointly directed by the *zongda* (civil leader), appointed by the government and the *ponlop* (religious authority), appointed by the *jekhenpo*. The agents

of royal and religious power are equally represented in the various councils. Each *zongkhag* is subdivided into sub-districts under the authority of *dungpa*, who are in charge of relations with the village chiefs, called *gap*, in the north, and *mandal*, in the south. A village chief supervises several villages whose councils are elected for a three-year term and where each family is represented by one of its members.

Over the course of centuries, the influence of the *zong* over the central power has never been opposed. They are still the keystone of the pyramidal structure of the Bhutanese sociocultural system. Their representatives, who transmit the esteemed opinions of the *zongda* and the *ponlop*, participate in elaborating government policy, and once decisions have been made, in seeing to it that they are applied. This surprising survival of feudal times is tending to falter because of unceasing administrative obstructions due to the ultra-conservativism and inefficiency of corrupt civil servants. The government, composed of the king (who must receive a vote of confidence from the As-

◀ *Archery is the national sport of the kingdom. There are numerous competitions. The archers are divided into two teams and compete by trying to hit a 23,5 x 8 inch target placed 492 feet away.*

This draft animal is the zo, a cross between a yak and an ox. It is hardy and
docile and perfectly adapted to work in altitudes up to 11,500 feet.

◄ Many houses, especially in the western part of the country, are decorated
with phallic symbols. This emblem of fertility and protection has been
inherited from Tantrism for which universal creation is a vast,
endlessly repeated act of copulation.

sembly every three years) and by two royal Councils to assist him, is trying, by means of incentives (promotions by merit, profit-sharing) or reinforced severity (harsher sentences in cases of fraud or corruption) to minimize the weaknesses of the system. Despite these efforts, it would seem that in the short run the system is condemned. In the south, it is under "democratic" pressure from the growing number of Indianized peoples (with a galloping demographic growth) who feel excluded from the political life of Bhutan.

The high valleys of northern and central Bhutan whose average elevation is between 5,900 and 9,000 feet enjoy a relatively mild climate. Farms are rich and consequently, nearly 70% of the Bhutanese live here.

During the summer rains, the rivers of northern and central Bhutan
(here, the Lhobrag) become veritable torrents, sweeping away everything
in their paths. Bridges are often simple, unstable footbridges
which have to be reconstructed every year.

The traditional Bhutanese dwelling consists of one or two storeys
(for the wealthier families). The animals are gathered on the ground floor
so that the family, which lives above, can benefit from their heat.

Sacred dances, only performed by monks, tell of events from the life of Buddha
or of the other important Buddhist saints. As here in Paro, they often mime
the confrontation between old demons and the spirits of the new faith.

Mealtime after a morning of prayer in Punakha monastery,
one of the oldest in the country. The jekhenpo and the highest dignitaries
live here. This community is very prestigious because it provides
the kingdom with most of its important dignitaries.

Each year, on the last morning of tsechu in Paro, the large thangka, Thongrol, measuring fifty feet on each side, is presented to the faithful to ward off the "five impurities". But it must be folded again before the first beam of sunlight rises above the horizon.

General view of the Paro zong, Rinchenpong, built by Drundrung, then restored by Zhabdrung in the 17th century. It was destroyed by fire in 1907 and reconstructed after the original plans. It contains the most precious manuscripts in Bhutan.

Traditional paintings, greatly inspired by Tantric mythology, use wrathful,
supernatural characters which are relics of pre-Buddhist demons.

The Tongsa zong is the seat of an important school of religious painting. Three novices, under the guidance of their "root-abbot" (on the left), give the finishing touches to a portrait of Guru Rinpoche holding a double dorje in his right hand.

The northern part of Arunachal Pradesh consists
of a long succession of mountains incised by deep glacial valleys.
A scattered population of semi-nomadic herders tend their poor livestock.
Here, not far from Jalaibaili Feny.

Arunachal Pradesh means "hill land of the rising sun", a poetic name which is only vaguely related to the actual coutryside. There is no resemblance whatsoever between the Himalayas hitherto visited. First of all, these mountains are much narrower, as if restricted by the course of the Brahmaputra. No longer is there a succession of regular foothills preceeding the heights of the Lesser Himalayas and then the peaks of the Great Himalayas. The Siwalik Hills have disappeared and the various massifs coalesce in one compact and hostile mass, incised by deep, mostly unexplored, valleys forged by powerful rivers that virtually drop onto the Assam piedmont.

A rugged, little known country

The Indians have been no more successful than the English colonists in dominating Arunachal Pradesh. During the era of the Indian Empire, people showed an interest in Assam, which was known for the high quality tea grown on its hills and which enjoyed the indisputable prestige drawn from the ancient culture of the kingdom of Kamarupa which had flourished there from the 4th to 13th centuries, before succumbing to the assaults of the Ahom, coming from Yunnan in China. Very little was known of the mysterious mountains bordering Assam on the north. Their summits were rarely visible. Rumor had it that in the territories known as the N.E.F.A. (*North East Frontier Agency*), the thick forest had both been cursed by the gods who forbade sunlight to enter it, and were inhabited by dangerous head-hunting savages. After Indian independence and the first conflicts with China, the N.E.F.A. began to arouse interest. As contact between the indigenous population and foreign or Indian visitors developed, it became obvious that these were peaceful, itinerant farming-hunting peoples with animist beliefs, rather than savages. On the other hand, rumor had not been mistaken as to climatic conditions. Nowhere else in the Himalayas does it rain as much. Certain lowlands have an annual rainfall of up to 275 inches!

For three-quarters of the year a thick fog shrouds the mountains below 9,800 feet. There is a thick tropical forest and luxuriant vegetation with innumerable species of epiphytes, orchids, mosses, ferns, bamboos and rhododendrons. In contrast with the overpopulated plains and hills of Assam (not geologically part of the Himalayas), the human presence in Arunachal Pradesh is minimal and houses are scattered.

Two zones should be distinguished: one consists of a narrow strip of frozen ground in the north, partially in Tibet; the other is entirely in Indian territory and it comprises all the land between 1,600 and 11,500 feet.

The first zone begins on the southern slopes of the Yarlung Tsangpo valley (the Tibetan name for the Brahmaputra) and rises to the summits of the central chain, dominated by two peaks that reach over 23,000 feet,

The land of the rising sun

Gyala Peri or Jialabaili Feng (25,446 feet) and Namcha Barva (23,461 feet), the highest unconquered mountain on earth. This austere landscape is impressive, especially past the Bomi valley where the Yigrong Chu rapids thunder down into the waters of the Tsangpo. Besides a few straggling villages, the region is practically uninhabited. No one lives above 14,800 feet. The power of the monsoons and the usual precipitation of tropical regions give rise to extreme climatic conditions (frequent landslides and snowstorms) that exclude human habitation. Between June and September, only the rare caravan from the east ventures over the mountain passes to the Tsangpo valley.

The few small farmers, some of whom have converted to Islam, lead a sedentary life eking out a living from meager mountain crops of barley and buckwheat. The absence of transhumant herdsman is unusual for Tibet, but can be explained by the fact that there are no meadows or grassy steppes, but only high altitude savannas without enough nutritive value to sustain livestock. To the far east, where the average elevation is lower, live seminomadic Tibetan peoples such as the Chingpo, the Lhardei or the Nasi, who have adapted Buddhist doctrine to their ancient shamanic traditions. These intermixed peoples, often referred to with disdain as *Lopa* ("savages") by other Tibetans, cultivate the low valleys by the slash-and-burn method. The three pillars of their society are a solid democratic tradition of equality among the different families, the absolute respect for customary rights and ancestor worship. Their wanderings often take them far beyond the Tibetan border, into China and Burma.

The second zone covers the greater part of northern Arunachal Pradesh. It is densely forested and harbors a remarkable mosaic of ethnic groups, although the total population figure is relatively low. The upper mountain regions are practically uninhabited. Most of the tribes are gathered in the lower or middle river valleys oriented north south that emerge in the Assam hills, especially in the Kameng, the Subansiri and the Siang, where the Brahmaputra flows. The Kameng delimits the geographical extent of Indian settlement. East of this valley, the eastern Himalayas should be considered as mountains of Southeast Asia. Few adequate ethnological studies have been carried out on these populations, most of whom are of Tibeto-Burmese origin in the east and Tibeto-Mongol origin in the north, with pre-Aryan "Indian" communities in the lowlands. Each tribe has its own language, culture and religious practices that it asserts in opposition to the others. This results in frequent inter-ethnic conflicts. The Hrusso have a feudal social system not unlike those of the Bhutanese, the Dafla divide themselves into rival clans, the Miri, the Mishing, the Adi (formerly called *Abor*, "savages") and further east, the Mishmi, the Khamti, the Sadiva, the Matak, the

Noktej and other Tsangla (or western Kachin), populations difficult to control that live on the Burmese border. Finally, to the south are many tribes related to the Assamese, they suffer from Indian acculturation even more than the others: the Bodo, the Garo, the Mikir who call themselves *Arleng* ("men"), the Khasi, the Wancho who are close to the Naga.

Except for certain very local groups such as the Apa Tani and some now sedentary Dafla who grow rice on an intensive basis, using hoes and highly irrigated paddies, most of the Arunachal Pradesh enthnic groups practice semi-itinerant slash-and-burn agriculture, called *jhum*. Mountain rice, millet, and corn are the main biannual harvests. They raise goats, pigs and gayal (B*os frontalis*), the latter more for sacrifices than for the meat. Animism is the rule; no major religion has managed to gain entry into these very conservative tribal systems. The belief in the spirits of nature and the permanent influence on the living of forces from the invisible world, condition the ancestor worship and the cult of the dead, who can be propitiated by frequent animal sacrifices. Authority is exercised by the council of the heads of families, often the oldest male members, aided by the shamans.

In the villages, communal houses large enough to shelter some ten families are used for occasional gatherings. This tribal system has been threatened since 1975 when the Indian government undertook to "civilize" the peoples it considered "savages," because of their different lifestyles. In order to do so, it encouraged the migration of colonists from Assam or Bengal, both Hindus and Muslims. So far, this normalization policy has caused a goodly number of revolts and much bloodshed, but has been relatively unsuccessful.

The Brahmaputra

Throughout the centuries the valley of the Brahmaputra has served as a thoroughfare for the Tibeto-Burmese and the Assamese. Until the middle of this century, it was considered one of the most dangerous places in the world, where the impenetrable countryside gave protection to threatening, war-like tribes. For a long time, its was believed that the Tibetan Tsangpo, whose source remained a mystery, and the Indian Brahmaputra, were two separate rivers. In the 19th century, however, Khintup, one of the Indian pundits, those explorer-spies sent out by the British to explore the Himalayas, proceeded up the Tsangpo and located its source in the glacier which covers the western slopes of Mount Kailasa.

At the end of the century, people began to suspect that the Tsangpo and the Brahmaputra might be one and the same river. A goodly number of European and Indian explorers tried to prove it and never reappeared. Newspapers at the time, of course, accused the riverside residents. Since then, the truth has been discovered. Their deaths were caused not by man, but by the very difficult survival conditions along the middle course of the Brahmaputra.

To this day, no one has ever followed the full length of the mythical 1,800 miles river from its source to its mouth. It is the highest river in the world and is fed by

some one hundred and twenty tributaries. It is known by different names, according to the region it flows through: it is called the Matsang Tsangpo and the Yarlung Tsangpo in Tibet, where its source lies at an altitude of 16,500 feet; in the Pei region, it takes on the name of Siang when it narrows suddenly in the midst of some splendid scenery and its wild, roaring waters are engulfed in narrow gorges over 3,200 feet deep, boxed in between the peaks of Gyala Peri and Namcha Barva. This is practically a virgin region where the river drops more than 6,500 feet in fewer than 125 miles. As it leaves the Himalayas, it widens and penetrates Assam where it becomes the Brahmaputra, before it irrigates Bangladesh where it is called the Yamuna, finally flows into the Bay of Bengal as the Meghna, after having received the waters of the Ganges.

The zone in the eastern Himalayas that it traverses is one of the least known in the world. Access is forbidden as much for political reasons (the many guerilla freedom fighters) and strategic reasons (since China claims much of the province), as for the real dangers the steep, hostile land represents. How to develop the potential energy of the Brahmaputra is another source of discord among India, Bangladesh and China. China is considering constructing one or several enormous dams on the river before it turns to the south. This would be the biggest generator of hydro-electric power in the world. India and Bangladesh, located downriver, look unfavorably upon this

The Brahmaputra has over one hundred tributaries. After thundering down Himalayan slopes through dizzing, steep gorges, many of them, such as the one pictured here, meander through the forested gap in Assam.

Chinese takeover, for the river belongs to them as well. But they do not agree on how the Brahmaputra is to be used once it enters the Assam plain. Delhi would like to harness the force of the river to produce electricity. Dacca would like to "tame" it so that Bangladesh will no longer be a victim of the flooding caused by the monsoons every year from June to September,

In the middle mountains, it rains for over nine months of the year. During the very rainy monsoon season, the countryside is engulfed in a permanent fog that the sun never seems able to penetrate.

when the river leaves its bed and inundates two-thirds of the country, killing hundreds of farmers and sending thousands of others, homeless onto the roads.

A controversial buffer zone

After an eventful history, the N.E.F.A. changed its name in 1971 to become Arunachal Pradesh. Since 1958 this Himalayan territory had been the center of serious military and political conflicts between China and India. The critical situation between these two great regional powers culminated in the lightning war of October 1962. The origin of the conflict dates back to the beginning of the century, in 1914, to be precise. The tripartite conference between Great Britain, China and India to settle boundary disputes in the Himalayas

225

was held in Shimla, the capital of Himachal Pradesh, in northwestern India. Laborious discussions finally led to the signing of a treaty that drew up the MacMahon line which was to serve as border between India and China. The latter, however, never officially recognized the demarcation line that extended from Ladakh to Assam, nor did it demonstrate any particular signs of

bellicosity. In 1954 the two nations signed a treaty of peaceful co-existence. The problem of the MacMahon line was not raised by the Chinese government, and in return, India recognized Beijing's sovereignty over Tibet, which it had annexed four years earlier. In 1958 - 1959, however, for domestic political reasons (the Cultural Revolution, orchestrated by the wife of Mao Zedong, was in full swing) as well as foreign political reasons (the Chinese were worried about the closer ties between the USSR and India) Communist China increased its verbal provocations and initiated border skirmishes in the eastern Himalayas where it claimed 12,800 square miles of Aksai Chin and all of the N.E.F.A., 34,750 square miles located south of the MacMahon line. Dissension increased between the

In the southern lowlands, one still finds some Adivasi, *peoples of pre-Aryan Mongol-Dravidian stock. They can be recognized by their very dark skin and the absence of any Negroid features.*

Here the Himalayan heights blend into the Mishmi range. This landscape ushers ▶ *in the dense vegetation of the southeast Asian tropical forests. The ochre-tinted mist that hangs over the countryside is caused by the slash-and-burn technique used to clear the forest and reclaim land suitable for cultivation.*

two countries. In 1962 Delhi decided not to renew the 1954 treaty as long as the problem of the border territories remained unsolved. On October 20th of that year, the Chinese army suddenly invaded Ladakh and the N.E.F.A. The Indian Prime Minister Nehru was taken by surprise and did not dispatch sufficient military forces to stop the invasion. The Indian army suffered a bitter defeat as the Chinese advanced towards Assam. The Western powers, particularly England and the United States, threatened to intervene, thus internationalizing the conflict. As if satisfied at having proven its military superiority, China proclaimed an unilateral cease-fire and ordered its troops to retreat towards the MacMahon line in the east, but kept Aksai Chin in the west, thus amputating an important part of Ladakh that India considered vital to its security. The problem has still not been settled, although tensions have lessened. Delhi is still intent on recuperating Aksai Chin and Beijing still claims the northern two-thirds of Arunachal Pradesh. Since then, both India and China have considerably increased their military presence in the mountains and have blocked off the entire area of the eastern Himalayas, reducing to a bare minimum the autonomy of the last small independent sovereign states of the Himalayas.

If, for the present, the international situation seems to be stabilized through the presence of opposing forces, the domestic trials of Arunachal Pradesh are far from over. Here, too, the present situation is the consequence of past events. In 1963, India, suspecting the local N.E.F.A. populations of being pro-Chinese, separated the region from the N.H.T.A. (*Naga Hills and Tuensang Area*, which became Nagaland) and added it to Assam. Chinese threats, as well as the violent ethnic clashes that immediately broke out, brought the Indian government to rescind its decision and grant the N.E.F.A. special status. Despite the "tough" government policy and the introduction of Indian colonists, tribal agitation has continued. Finally, in 1972 the N.E.F.A. became Arunachal Pradesh, a territory with a special status within the Indian Union. Today, it is the least developed province of the country. Illiteracy reaches 88% and life expectancy is less than fifty years. The dark, still predominantly virgin, forests of

Big herds of gayal (Bos frontalis) are common in the lowlands on the Assam border, here in Dafla country, inhabited by Tibeto-Burmese ethnic groups. These powerful, easily domesticated animals, along with pigs and goats, comprise the people's principal wealth.

*Arunachal Pradesh long remained isolated from the other regions of India.
Daily life here provides numerous examples of how far behind they lag.
These fishermen from the Lohit district use the same hoop nets their distant
ancestors did over a thousand years ago.*

The southern foothills of Arunachal Pradesh are covered with tea plantations. ▶
*Even if their reputation is not that of Darjeeling or Sikkim,
most Indian teas come from this area or neighboring Assam, where they grew
wild long before Chinese species were imported.*

the region are the scene of continual inter-ethnic conflicts and harbor various guerilla groups backed by Russia, China or the West. Having learned from its past experiences, India now keeps its eyes riveted on the eastern Himalayan crestline. Arunachal Pradesh has had to bear the brunt of India's fears. It is armed to the teeth and has practically become a forbidden

The Kameng and Subansiri districts are inhabited by small, rival ethnic groups. Here, in this Miri village of seminomadic hunter-gatherers, the people are animists and practice a sort of itinerant subsistence farming based on slash-and-burn techniques.

zone. Indians need a special permit to go there and only the rare foreigner can obtain a pass in Delhi, and it then has to be confirmed by the army in the province. Only a few foolhardy adventurers have tried to travel without the required authorizations. Woe be to those who are caught, for they are systematically considered to be spies and are sentenced to long prison terms. This politico-military quarantine explains the region's considerable economic underdevelopment and the fragmentary information that geographers, ethnologists, zoologists and botanists have at their disposal. The "land of the rising sun" runs the risk of remaining for years to come the "cellar of the Himalayas", as its inhabitants call it.

A Minyong woman bringing branches and leaves to repair the roof of her house in the Siang valley. She belongs to an eastern clan related to the Tibeto-Burmese ethnic group, the Adi, which, until the seventies, were pejoratively called Abor (savages).

The soil is most fertile in the lower valleys. Indians and Bengalis have been flocking here, attracted by the mirage of new lands and thus becoming a lumpen proletariat, easily exploited by the big landowners. (Here, in Lohit).

Abridged Bibliography

AUBOYER J.
Dieux et démons de l'Himalaya, Paris, 1977.
BLOFELD J.
Le Bouddhisme tantrique du Tibet, Paris, 1976.
BRINES R.
The Indo-Pakistani Conflict, London, 1965.
CHENEVIERE A.
Bhutan, royaume d'Himalaya, Paris, 1989.
DAVID-NEEL A.
Magic and Mystery in Tibet, New York, 1971.
DENIS J.
Les Clefs de l'Himalaya, Paris, 1986.
FRÉDÉRIC L.
Dictionnaire de la civilisation indienne, Paris, 1987.
FUKADA K.
The Great Himalayas, New York, 1973.
GONDA J.
Les Religions de l'Inde I et II, Paris, 1962 and 1965.
GRIFFITH W.
*Travels in Assam, Burma, Afghanistan
and the neighbouring countries*, Delhi, 1982.
INGHOLT H.
Gandharan Art in Pakistan, New York, 1957.
JAIN G.
India meets China in Nepal, New York, 1964.

LEIFER W.
Himalaya, Mountains of Destiny, London, 1962.
LOUDE J.-Y.
Kalash, les derniers « infidèles » de l'Hindou-Koush, Paris, 1980.
NICOLSON N.
L'Himalaya, Paris, 1975.
POLUNIN O. AND STAINTON A.
Flowers of the Himalaya, Oxford, 1984.
REID R.
The Frontier Areas bordering in Assam, Shillong, 1942.
RICHARDSON H. AND SNELLGROVE D.
A Cultural History of Tibet, London, 1968.
RUSTOMJI N.
*Enchanted Frontiers, Sikkim, Bhutan and India's North-Eastern
Borderlands*, Calcutta, 1973.
SCHALLER G.
Les Pierres du silence, la recherche de la faune himalayenne, Paris, 1980.
SIDDIQUI K.
Conflict, Crisis and War in Pakistan, London, 1972.
SING M.
L'Art de l'Himalaya, UNESCO, Paris, 1979.
TENZIN GYATSO
L'Enseignement du Dalaï Lama. La clef du Madhyamika, Paris, 1976.
TUCCI G.
Théorie et pratique du mandala, Paris, 1974.

◀ *"Sunset over the waters of the lake (Lake Dal) is like a woman's cool kiss
on a feverish brow", goes the old Moghul adage. The calm beauty of
the lake and its surrounding gardens on a mild spring evening
only confirms the truth of the saying.*

Himachal Pradesh in the beginning of summer, in the Shimla region, when the monsoons begin to strike the southern side of the mountains. The slopes are plunged into a cocoon-like atmosphere caused by the abundant rainfalls which evaporate during the hot days.

Kashmir, which is unfortu- ▶▶ nately torn apart today by political events, is a country of numerous assets. It has a mild climate, even in winter, and some of the most fertile soil on the continent. The villagers bring in two harvests a year.

Printing
EGEDSA
Rois de Corella, 12, 16, Nave 1
08205 Sabadell /Barcelone

© 1998 VILO -
25 rue Ginoux - 75015 Paris
All rights reserved throughout the world

Printed in October 1998
at Sabadell (Spain) on the EGEDSA press
ISBN 2 71910493-0